# FINANCIAL SURVIVAL
for the
# 21st Century

Graydon G. Watters

# Additional Praise
## for Financial Survival for the 21st Century

**JEFFREY A. SMITH**
C.G.A.
Manager, Profit
Sharing and Stock
Purchase
Administration
Canadian Tire
Corporation, Ltd.

❝ FINANCIAL SURVIVAL FOR THE **21**st CENTURY condenses all of the elements of its predecessors FINANCIAL PURSUIT and LIFESTYLE PURSUIT into an easy to read and understand retirement planning tool. I recommend it to all Canadians who have a desire to take charge of their journey toward retirement. ❞

**PIERRE BOILEAU**
Vice President
Human Resources
JDS FITEL INC.

❝ Graydon's insight and knowledge are truly at the forefront of the **21**st Century. It is obvious that he is concerned for the individual. He is determined to provide an understanding of financial security and how to attain it. This book is well written, easy to understand and a must read for any hard working Canadian! ❞

**MACLEANS**

❝ The key ingredients in successful investing are knowledge, time, temperament and money. "Even I don't have the four ingredients anymore. That's why most investors need an advisor - they're too busy and they don't have the time to learn everything they need to know." ❞

**DAVID CLEMENT**
Manager —
Pensions &
Human Resources
Projects
Campbell Soup
Company Ltd.

❝ FINANCIAL SURVIVAL FOR THE **21**st CENTURY is the latest important educational contribution by Graydon Watters. It is a handbook which clearly outlines why there is an important need for everyone to have an investment plan in place today. I highly recommend it for anyone who does not have a personal plan and wants a quick starting point to develop a strategy and plan, and for anyone else who wants an eye-opening refresher on the issues of the day and basic investment concepts. ❞

66 If I had the opportunity to learn Graydon's secrets 20 years ago, I would have retired, comfortably, at age fifty. My children will not miss out on the opportunity to learn Graydon's secrets now. This book is a "must have" for anyone interested in controlling their destiny through FINANCIAL SURVIVAL FOR THE 21st CENTURY. 99

CAROL ARCHINOFF
Gainsharing Coordinator
Allied Signal
Aerospace Canada

66 Your powerful presentation skills and incredible wealth of knowledge in the area of financial planning made your recent seminar presentation to our employee's an overwhelming success. FINANCIAL SURVIVAL FOR THE 21st CENTURY should compound this success! 99

RON F. SUTER
Employee Relations
Association
Ford Motor
Company of
Canada, Limited

66 I have consistently received high praise from employees at financial planning seminars for Financial Pursuit and Lifestyle Pursuit. This financial and retirement planning material is very readable, understandable, practical, and most importantly, relevant to the average Canadian. Like FINANCIAL PURSUIT and LIFESTYLE PURSUIT, FINANCIAL SURVIVAL FOR THE 21st CENTURY should be a real winner. 99

ROSS BROWN
Vice President,
Human Resources
TVX Gold Inc.

66 FINANCIAL SURVIVAL FOR THE 21st CENTURY is an excellent resource for all employees. We always look forward to having you facilitate our seminars. Your exciting approach to financial planning is both informative and refreshing. Graydon, I'm sure your new book will be a great success for you. 99

DEBORAH BROWN
Assistant Personnel
Manager — Canada
State Farm Insurance
Companies

66 The 1980's was a decade of spending, the 1990's is a decade of reflection, and the 2000's will be the decade for personal saving and investing. FINANCIAL SURVIVAL FOR THE 21st CENTURY is timely in its discussion of the major paradigm shifts affecting employment, pensions, and retirement issues. This book is an extremely valuable resource for employees. 99

BARRY A. BRACKLEY
Administrative
Services
Toyota Canada Inc.

*The author wishes to express thanks and appreciation to Towers Perrin, an international human resource consulting firm who granted permission to use their material.*

Film,Print and Bind: Best Book Manufacturers

Printed and bound in Canada

Copy Editor: Susan Wallace-Cox

Design: Bold Graphic Communication Ltd.

**Canadian Cataloguing in Publication Data**

Watters, Graydon G., 1943–

    Financial survival for the 21st century

    ISBN 0-9681285-0-5

    1. Finance, Personal. 2. Investments.

I. Financial Knowledge Inc. II. Title.

HG179.W39 1997    332.024'01    C97-930444-X

**Disclaimer**

The information contained herein has been obtained from sources which we believe reliable but we cannot guarantee its accuracy or completeness. This book is not and under no circumstances is to be construed as an offer to sell or the solicitation of an offer to buy any securities. This book is furnished on the basis and understanding that Financial Knowledge Inc. is to be under no responsibility or liability whatsoever in respect thereof. The author/publisher would welcome any further information pertaining to errors or omissions in order to make corrections in subsequent editions.

# Table of
# Contents

# Foreword

**W**e all have a personal definition of success. The role that financial security plays in our success may vary with each of us, but one thing is certain: getting a firm handle on our financial future is critical to us all.

*Financial Survival for the 21st Century* by Graydon Watters is a book for anyone interested in first understanding the many and often complex investment options available today and then adapting them to meet their unique financial goals. For new investors, it's a useful, step-by-step guide to getting started. For experienced investors, it should serve as a terrific resource and planning tool.

At Fidelity Investments, we have always believed that professional advisors can help investors become more knowledgeable. That's why we created the Fidelity Institute: to give financial advisors the most advanced learning tools possible to better serve their clients.

The Institute's commitment to lifelong learning is a major reason we decided to sponsor this special edition of *Financial Survival for the 21st Century*. It clearly describes important financial planning topics ranging from mutual fund investing to how to build a personal financial strategy with the help of your financial advisor.

I invite you to read this book, then talk to your financial advisor about how these concepts can be put to work for you. It will be time well-spent, today and in the future.

Kevin Kelly
President and Chief Executive Officer
Fidelity Investments Canada Limited

# Preface

The information age has arrived, causing major paradigm shifts. Work and employment will never be the same — old-line manufacturing is on the wane, while new-age technologies and the knowledge revolution are on the rise.

The old type of corporate-sponsored pension plans are quickly becoming a thing of the past — employers are consistently passing more control over to employees.

Government-sponsored social security programs are shifting gears — away from universal programs to programs based on need.

It has been documented in recent years that very few Canadians retire with financial security. It is our belief that during the next two decades the financial planning industry will emerge as a major force to enable more Canadians to take charge of their financial health and to retire with dignity. In fact, by the year 2000, financial planning education will be one of the greatest growth industries in the country and will be well entrenched as a middle-class phenomenon.

Retirees represent an increasing percentage of the Canadian population. The active workforce, which historically has supported retirees, is shrinking. During the next two decades the entire baby-boom generation will reach retirement age. This will create an inverse pyramid, whereby a smaller working population will have to support a very large group of retired citizens.

Some people are predicting intergenerational conflict — there appears to be an increasing reluctance, inability, and outright unwillingness by government and younger Canadians to support the massive boomer generation heading for retirement. The federal government has promised a review of all income transfer programs and a debate on the Canadian pension system. Common sense suggests that something will have to give.

Beginning in 2001, a new tax-free monthly Seniors Benefit will replace OAS, GIS, and the age and pension income tax credits. Eligibility for the Seniors Benefit will be based on a couple's combined income and will be phased out for those with higher incomes.

The 21st Century will produce an even greater disparity between those who have and those who have not.

For those who have the foresight to plan for the future, retirement can be the best time of your life. On the other hand, it can be a major disappointment for those who fail to prepare. This is the purpose of this handbook. We know that if you take charge of your cash flow today, if you understand the difference between saving and investing, if you recognize the different types and degrees of risk, and if you apply a *winning* mental attitude to the management of your pension funds and other financial assets, retirement with financial security will be your trophy.

# The dawning of the information age

is upon us. ● Computers and the microchip

**GREATEST IMPACT ON MANKIND** **PAST:** PRINTING PRESS ● AUTOMOBILE ● TELEPHONE ● TELEVISION

have changed the world forever and the

**PRESENT:** INTERNET ● COMPUTERS ● GENETIC ENGINEERING ● BIOMEDICAL ENGINEERING

pace is accelerating. Interactive television

**FUTURE:** SUPER-CONDUCTORS ● NANOTECHNOLOGY ● OPTICAL COMPUTERS ● VOICE ACTIVATED COMPUTERS

via cable or satellite has arrived. ● These

"New technologies are

tremendous advances in technology and

replacing workers so quickly

telecommunications are driving us from the

that modern economies will

industrial manufacturing economy we used to

soon be able to run smoothly

know towards a service-based knowledge

using the labour of only a

economy. ● The gold watch earned for a life-

fraction of their citizens."

time of corporate service and cradle to grave

— Jeremy Rifkin

security benefits are now recent history.

# one

# Planning for the 21st Century

**1**

**I**n the year 1900 the average life expectancy for Canadian males was 49 years; for women 47 years, many of whom lost their lives in childbirth. By the year 2000 the average life expectancy for Canadian men will be about mid 70s, and for women early 80s. Our potential lifespans have almost doubled during the last century and we continue to add one to one-and-a-half years every decade.

How much financial planning did the average individual do back in the year 1900? None! The plan for most people was to work until the day they died. They literally died with their boots on. Yesterday's employee worked a lifetime for one company and received a company pension. Tomorrow's employee will work for a number of companies and take charge of creating a pension for themselves. Today's employees often find themselves caught between the extremes of an employer's paternalistic patronage and the necessity of having to control their own destiny by creating a survival-of-the-fittest plan for their future retirement.

The management of one's career, financial, lifestyle, and retirement pursuits seemed so simple just a few years ago. You went to school, perhaps college or university, found a job, and worked for the same company for thirty plus years until retirement. Then you would live a life of leisure using accumulated pensions and savings as your source of income until death did you part. But this was prior to the high tech information revolution.

Now technological change enables a company to do more with less, which causes unstable conditions in the workforce. And the older the worker, the greater the effect. During the last decade, virtually every major corporation has experienced some form of downsizing, rightsizing, or right-aging, and for the foreseeable future they will continue to restructure, re-engineer, outsource, and form new strategic alliances. The greatest effect in this upheaval has been on the older worker. Obviously, the older worker is more expensive to carry on the payroll and so the emphasis has been to keep the younger, less-expensive worker employed. Unfortunately, many older workers find themselves unemployed and lacking the resources to enjoy a comfortable retirement, and in many cases, having to tap into what little savings they have managed to accumulate. What a travesty of justice in an age when people are living longer, healthier, and more productive lives!

## Canadians are Overly Optimistic

Canadians are overly optimistic about their retirement dreams and most are grossly lacking adequate planning to achieve their retirement goals. Numerous research polls validate this statement. In our seminars and workshops it is the rule rather that the exception that 75% of participants do not have clear, concise, focused goals pertaining to their retirement needs.

Towers Perrin, an international human resource consulting firm, recently completed a survey that produced some real eye-openers. Some of the highlights from this survey include:

- Three-quarters of working Canadians believe their standard of living after retirement will be the same or better than it was before retirement.
- Three-quarters are also doing little or no planning for retirement.
- Most Canadians expect to retire before age 65.
- Three-quarters acknowledge that it will be their own responsibility to provide a major portion of their retirement income.
- As many as one in two working Canadians are saving less than $2000 annually, including contributions to their employer's pension plan.
- More than three-quarters say they do not receive enough help from their employer to plan for retirement.

Most of the survey participants would qualify as part of the baby boom generation. So let's look at some boomer facts:

**9 million boomers born in Canada between 1947 and 1966**

Age in 1997

| | 31 | 40.5 | 50 | |
| --- | --- | --- | --- | --- |
| | YOUNGEST | MIDDLE | OLDEST | |

For those boomers who do plan, their top three goals are listed as home ownership, education funding, and retirement planning. Unlike the previous generation, today's boomers will have to amass significantly greater financial resources on their own in order to achieve their goals.

Although the cost of living generally increases in line with the Consumer Price Index during one's working years, most families experience three major decreases in their personal cost of living index during their lifetime.

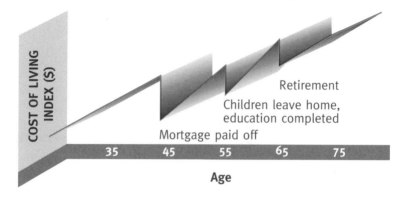

So the question is "How realistic is your retirement-age goal and have you made the appropriate plans to reach this goal?" Your retirement-age goal will depend upon when your working career began, when you bought your home, and at what age you raised your family. For example, if you leave your job at age 57, instead of age 62, your annual income might be 25% to 30% less. There is a substantial difference in income at retirement if you leave early because:

- you have five years less earnings
- you are contributing for five years less to your pension
- you have five years additional drawings on your pension

## The Employer/Employee Relationship is Redefined

The global recession and the re-engineered high-tech workplace have redefined the social contract between the employer and the employee in two major ways during the last decade:

**1** **job security**          **2** **pension benefits**

In the past it was not uncommon for an employee to work for one company for a lifetime. Today's employee does not have this security. By necessity people must be willing to move freely from company to company. Perhaps the bigger issue is pensions, which are often seen as an expendable luxury rather than a necessary benefit.

Today's employee needs to apply a radical change in thinking. This involves a paradigm shift of responsibility from the traditional pattern of the past in which an employee relied on the paternalistic behaviour of an employer to one in which the employee assumes responsibility for his or her own future.

## A New Paradigm for Retirement is Required

| OLD SYSTEM | | NEW SYSTEM |
| --- | --- | --- |
| 20th Century | | 21st Century |
| paternalism | ● | survivalist |
| focus on employer | ● | focus on employee |
| someone else's responsibility | ● | your responsibility |

| PENSIONS PAST | | PENSIONS FUTURE |
| --- | --- | --- |
| Government Pensions | ❶ | Employee Savings & Investments |
| Employer Pensions | ❷ | Employer Pensions |
| Employee Savings & Investments | ❸ | Government Pensions |
| | ❹ | Continuous Paid Work |

What is required of today's employee? The 21st century employee must adopt a survivalist attitude. He or she must be centered, must accept responsibility, and must refocus and determine the actual goals of retirement. He or she should be prepared to work full time until age 60 and part-time thereafter.

Consider the fact that every day worked adds money to your retirement fund and reduces, by one day, the amount of time in which to spend your hard earned cash once you do retire. Your challenge is to determine exactly how much you will need in order to be financially stable and at what point you stop spending for today and start saving for tomorrow.

Most retirees can live **comfortably** on 70% of their | pre-retirement income. | However,

those with low pre-retirement incomes may need

100% and the extremely wealthy much less than

"I don't know what your destiny will be,

70%. ■ The 1997 federal | deficit | is projected to be

but one thing I know; the only ones

$19 billion; it is simply the difference between rev-

among you who will be really happy

enue and spending. ■ Your share of the $800 bil-

are those who will have sought and

lion accumulated federal and provincial debt is

found a way to serve others."

$27,500. ■ The amount and kind of work available

— Dr. Albert Schweitzer

for | future retirees | will depend on their level of

RETIREMENT OF THE TYPE THAT HAS BEEN THE ACCEPTED

formal and practical education as well as specific

NORM OF THE 20TH CENTURY IS NOW A GRAND ILLUSION.

skills to match the information-age technologies.

# two

# Retirement —
# The Opportunity Of A Lifetime

**2**

**A**t the turn of this century we witnessed a mass exodus from the country to the city as Canadians found employment in the manufacturing and industrial economies. The shift from an agricultural society to an industrial nation brought numerous benefits, particularly in the nature of work. Mass production, increased productivity, and better health and living conditions led companies to the concept of initiating retirement as a reward for years of service. The previous generation expected a working career spanning 40 to 45 years, retirement at age 65, and a life expectancy of seven to ten years in retirement.

Two major shifts have occurred since the previous generation approached retirement:

**1** We are living longer, healthier lives, adding one to two years to our life cycle every decade.

**2** We are retiring earlier, often in our mid to late 50s.

The major problem employees face today is an "entitlement mindset." Based on the examples set by their fathers and grandfathers, employees began to equate years of hard work with a retirement sponsored by the government and by their employer.

Today, nothing could be further from the truth. It is not the responsibility of the government or employers; the ultimate responsibility belongs to the employee. There is no such thing as entitlement in the corporate world — the buck really does stop with you.

## Freedom 55 — Myth or Reality?

Two of the greatest myths surrounding a retirement with dignity involve the concepts of leisure and financial stability.

Most Canadians perceive retirement as a time of leisure, recreation, and relaxation — a time to enjoy the fruits of one's labour. In reality it is a time of major adjustment to one's lifestyle and financial well-being.

So who is responsible for perpetuating the leisure myth? The advertising industry! Probably one of the most successful electronic media ad slogans ever developed was "Freedom 55" for London Life. Most Canadians are very aware of this ad and the concept it preaches of being financially free at age 55. But that's not all. Take a close look at the ad — the backdrop is a beach, the sun is shining, the surf is up, there is a couple walking along the beach hand in hand, smiling, enjoying the good life. But wait, take a close look at this couple, supposedly age 55. What's the notion being presented here. Not only can you be financially free at age 55, you can look 35 when you get there, you have no signs of aging — no wrinkles, no excess body weight, no obvious signs of hair loss. Where is reality?

## Six Major Resources at Retirement

The financial myth involves the "Six Major Resources" Canadians rely on to fund their retirements. These resources can be viewed as part of a three-legged stool:

### SIX MAJOR RESOURCES AT RETIREMENT

**GOVERNMENT**

1. Old Age Security (OAS)
2. Canada Pension Plan (CPP)

**EMPLOYER**

3. Registered Pension Plan (RPP)

**EMPLOYEE**

4. RRSPs
5. Personal Investments
6. Home

Government programs were designed to provide approximately 40% of your financial needs at retirement; 15% would be provided by Old Age Security (OAS) and up to 25% from the Canada Pension Plan (CPP). To the extent that an individual was not entitled to the maximum from these two sources, and if they had no other source of income, they might also be entitled to a Guaranteed Income Supplement (GIS) to bring them to a basic minimum subsistence income level.

## Government Debt —The Harsh Reality

Government benefits have become increasingly suspect during the last few years. Universal programs such as Old Age Security (OAS) and the age and pension tax credits will be replaced by the new Seniors Benefit beginning in 2001. It is a means tested approach to benefits based on a couple's combined income and will be phased out for those with higher incomes. Quite simply, governments are broke and there is no easy fix. The federal and provincial debt in Canada is approximately $800 billion. That is bad enough in itself but we owe over $340 billion of that sum to other countries. And on any given day, the countries lending us money can shut off the taps.

### Canada's Debt — $ Billions

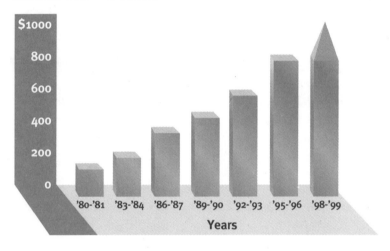

### G7 Countries—Net Foreign Debt—1996

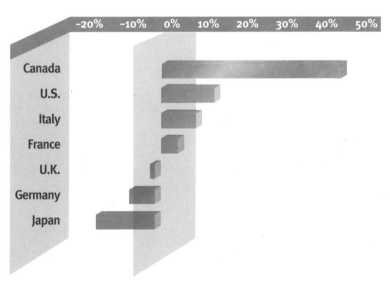

## Three Classes of Activity in Retirement

A balanced lifestyle for most Canadian employees requires three major classes of activity in retirement — leisure, part-time or full-time paid work, and volunteerism in order to lead a fulfilling and self-satisfying life.

The hard facts are:

- We could find ourselves in a retirement that might last longer than our previous working careers.
- Most people are not financially able to pursue a meaningful retirement that could last two or three decades.

Retirement, as this generation has come to expect it, has become unaffordable for most Canadians. Life expectancies that could take us into our 80s and 90s dictate two new mindsets for today's 30 to 50-year-olds:

1. Plan on working full-time as close to age 60 as possible and gradually reduce to part-time status right into your 70s.

2. Maintain a more aggressive growth allocation with your investments for at least two additional decades, otherwise you run the risk of running out of money before you run out of retirement.

Most successful retirees combine two or all three retirement activities of leisure, paid-work, and volunteerism to provide a satisfying retirement lifestyle.

In 1966 CPP premiums were 3.6% of pensionable earnings with employees and companies each paying half. Contribution levels in 1997 have been revised to 6.0% and they will rise to 9.9% during the next 6 years to keep the system from going bankrupt. One of the major drains on the CPP is that currently, 300,000 people are receiving an average of $650 a month for disabilities. 30% of all healthcare expenses occur during the final 30 days of life, regardless of the age of the patient.

"The period between 1995 and 2030 will see the number of those aged 60 plus in Canada rise by 155% to become the overwhelming majority of the population. Most because of poor planning will have to work at least until 70 years of age. At least 30% will end up in poverty."

— Jerry White

# three

# Pensions — Government Plans

**3**

**C**hanging demographics, with 25% of Canadians reaching the age of 65 or older by the year 2036, will have a dramatic impact on the Government's ability to fund the country's social security programs. Therefore, all universal programs need to be subject to a means test due to the rapidly aging population.

The Federal government recently announced a sweeping overhaul of the OAS system and the GIS replacing them with a Seniors Benefit beginning in 2001. At the same time, the age credit for those 65 and older and the pension income credit will be eliminated. Eligibility for the Seniors Benefit will be based on a couple's combined income. A single senior with about $52,000 in other income or a couple with $78,000 joint income will lose the benefit entirely.

OAS began in 1952, based on a residency test, and paid $40 per month at age 70, or means tested pensions of $40 per month between ages 65 and 69. When introduced, life expectancies were under age 70 for men and just over age 70 for women so that ordinarily, the Government only had to pay for a very short time. Now with life expectancies in the mid 70s to early 80s, OAS payments are often made for one to two decades.

**Life Expectancies – Old Age Security, Canada Pension Plan**

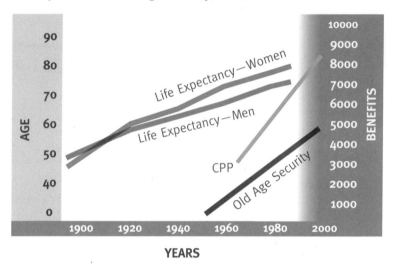

**YEARS**

CPP may not fare much better than OAS. Originally introduced in 1966, CPP was not fully funded at the start. It was funded on a pay-as-you-go basis with a two year cushion. CPP currently has an unfunded liability of $1.2 trillion, 50% more than the federal and provincial debt combined.

Today's retirees receive the CPP benefit at a ratio of 6 to 1 for every dollar contributed. Unless there is a radical change to the plan, the most a person who is midway through their working career today can hope to receive in the future is $1 back for each $1 contributed.

| Date of Birth | Each $1.00 CPP contribution will purchase a future benefit of: |
| --- | --- |
| 1920 | $7.00 |
| 1960 | $2.60 |
| 1997 | $1.00 |

CPP is based on employment earnings and mandatory contributions are split between employer and employee. The plan pays retirement, death, and disability benefits at age 65 or as early as age 60 after a minimum of one year of contributions. Employees must make maximum contributions for 85% of the period since 1966 to receive maximum benefit or the benefit will be reduced. The maximum benefit is 25% of the Average Industrial Wage or the Year's Maximum Pensionable Earnings (YMPE) in your last three years.

Major pension reforms are required to offset a shrinking workforce and an aging population. The proportion of those over age 65 has increased from 7.8% in 1951, to 11.6% in 1991, and is expected to reach 25% by 2036.

**Canada's Aging Population**

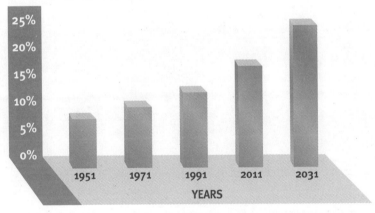

A major study on aging and pension reform conducted by the government during 1994 — 1997 will likely result in many additional pension reforms and the age for retirement increased to age 67 or possibly 69.

**100%** of public sector employees have

| Insurance Company Projection | Financial Knowledge Inc. Projection |
|---|---|
| Age 45 in 1982 to Age 65 in 2002 | Age 45 in 1997 to Age 65 in 2017 |

employer pension plans. **31%** of private

| 11% | FINANCIALLY INDEPENDENT | 11% |
|---|---|---|

sector employees have employer pension

| 8% | STILL WORKING | 30% |
|---|---|---|

plans. On average **45%** of all Canadians

| 38% | WILL HAVE DIED | 24% |
|---|---|---|

have employer pension plans. **80%** of the

| 43% | LIVING AT SUBSISTENCE LEVEL | 35% |
|---|---|---|

population simply **cannot afford**

to retire because they are not prepared

financially. The ultimate responsibility

for your retirement belongs **only** to **you**.

# four

# Pensions —
# Corporate Plans

**4**

**W**hat is a pension plan? The purpose of a pension plan is to deliver a fixed or indexed benefit that will provide a reasonable standard of living for the remainder of your lifetime after you retire. The pension plan is a procedural tool that allows the accumulation of money by an employer, an employee, or both, on a tax-free basis until retirement. At that point it will be taxable as it is withdrawn, but usually, at a lower rate.

## Company Pension Plans — Registered Pension Plans (RPPs)

Most major companies in Canada offer registered pension plans (RPPs) for their employees. These plans vary widely according to:

- percentage of income contributed
- retirement age
- indexing of payments
- payments to spouse in the event of death
- additional benefits of the plan, such as disability, death insurance, etc.
- vesting — the time you have to work before the plan becomes guaranteed
- portability, or the ease with which you can shift your accumulated financial credit from one plan to another

## Defined Benefit Plans (DB)

The majority of private RPPs are of the defined benefit type. With these plans, your benefits are calculated on a formula, based on earnings and length of service. Three main types of defined benefit plans include Flat Benefit Plans, Career Average Plans, and Final Average Plans.

The latter type is the most common and is based on a formula that provides automatic updating; you receive a pension such as 1.5% of your average earnings multiplied by the number of years worked, and based on your last three to five years of employment. For example, if you belonged to a defined benefit/final average plan and worked for the same company for 30 years, your annual pension income would be similar to the following:

| Earnings During the Last Five Years | | Pension |
|---|---|---|
| 1992 | $ 34,000 | $194,000 |
| 1993 | 36,000 | ÷ 5 |
| 1994 | 39,000 | = $38,800 |
| 1995 | 41,000 | X 1.5 |
| 1996 | 44,000 | X 30 years |
| | $194,000 | = $17,460 |

## Defined Contribution Plans (DC)

An increasingly popular alternative to the defined benefit plan is the defined contribution plan, or money purchase plan. These plans provide a pension based on the amount of accumulated funds available at the time the pension is to commence; they do not guarantee a specific benefit level. Contributions by the employer and employee accumulate in a fund and, depending on what the fund is worth at retirement, the contributions are used to purchase an annuity, a life income fund (LIF), a locked-in RRSP, a locked-in retirement account (LIRA), or similar plan.

## Haves Versus Have Nots

Less than one out of two Canadians are covered by Registered Pension Plans with their employers. The typical private sector worker is currently saving less than 7% in corporate pension plans and RRSPs, according to the Canadian Institute of Actuaries. To ensure adequate retirement income, they should be saving at a rate of 12% to 16% per year.

Most DB pensions average a payout of between 20% and 50% of the best three to five years salary. According to the actuarial study, this payout will not be adequate for a retirement that could stretch over 20 to 35 years. Couple this with the fact that Government pensions such as OAS and CPP cannot be relied upon and the employee is left with **only one sure bet** — to maximize his or her personal pensions and investments, using procedural tools such as Registered Retirement Savings Plans (RRSPs), Registered Retirement Income Funds (RRIFs), Life Income Funds (LIFs), and Locked-in Retirement Accounts (LIRAs) to mention a few. We'll discuss these later. The bottom line is the buck stops with the individual.

## Defined Contribution Plans Will Experience Exponential Growth Over the Next Decade

DC plans are designed to meet the needs of today's employee who is much more mobile and therefore requires greater flexibility. Major improvements to pension legislation during the last few years, concerning vesting, portability, and tax considerations are rapidly making DC the pension of choice for many employees.

Currently there is a trend among employers to review, restructure, and upgrade their existing pension plans. More and more companies are moving away from DB to DC plans or supplementing existing plans with money purchase plans or Group Registered Retirement Savings Plans (GRSPs). In the process, more of the responsibility for decision-making is being placed on the employee's shoulders.

## Weighing Your Pension Plan Alternatives

### Defined Benefit (DB)
- of interest to longer-service employees
- provides a clearly defined benefit that reflects your earnings, pensionable years of service, and your age at retirement
- less contribution room for RRSP
- survivor protection limited to death benefit under DB
- greater security, no volatility risk as pension benefit is guaranteed, regardless of pension plan performance
- your tolerance for risk — asset allocation and investment decisions are made for you

### Defined Contribution (DC)
- usually better for shorter-service employees
- provides a defined amount of company contributions
- dollar value in plan is known but account value at retirement is unknown
- more contribution room for RRSP for most employees
- administration and record-keeping is easily understood
- survivor benefit can be greater with defined contribution plan
- greater risk, short-term volatility, but potential for long-term growth; employee decides how to allocate assets
- the amount of pension benefit received is based on how long the employee is in the plan, earnings on contributions, age, and interest rates at the time pension commences
- often provides greater flexibility on how pension benefits are paid at retirement

Other such capital accumulation or money purchase plans include Deferred Profit Sharing Plans (DPSPs) or Group Registered Retirement Savings Plans (GRSPs) and various profit-sharing arrangements. The investment risks with these pensions also shifts from the employer or plan sponsor to the employee or plan members.

## Deferred Profit Sharing Plan (DPSP)

This pension plan is very similar to a defined contribution plan, however, employer contributions vary according to the company's profitability. The plan is designed to encourage employee interest and loyalty in the company's growth prospects and future potential. In theory this type of plan creates a win-win situation, whereby if the company is successful, the employee will be rewarded.

## Major Benefits For Making Group RSP Contributions

When an employer empowers an employee to take more control over his or her affairs, several major benefits are apparent:

- pay yourself first
- payroll deduction
- diversification by assets
- savings not locked-in under pension legislation
- professional management
- flexibility and portability
- no need to borrow
- direct reporting — statements
- immediate tax savings
- dollar cost averaging
- ease of management
- no large sum required at RSP deadline
- spousal income splitting
- focused retirement goals
- diversification of investments

We'll expand on these benefits in later chapters.

# Survey of Workshop Participants—Ages 27 to 50
## From FKI Financial Knowledge Inc. Corporate Programs

**65%** feel they are not saving enough for retirement

**50%** remain optimistic they'll have adequate funds for retirement

**60%** feel they need help in planning for retirement

**80%** cite their employer-sponsored pension plan as their top source of retirement income

**80%** of participants supplement their employer's pension plan with RRSP contributions

**15%** have experience with equities (stock) ownership

**30%** have experience with equity mutual funds

**90%** list their greatest concern as "how to find a financial planner"

**70%** list their second greatest concern as fees and commission costs

**40%** expect to work at least part-time during retirement

"Youth is the time of getting, middle age of improving, and old age of spending; a negligent youth is usually attended by an ignorant middle age, and both by an empty old age."

— Anne Bradstreet

OUR WORLD ECONOMY IS INCREASINGLY AN ECONOMY OF THE MIND, AN ECONOMY DOMINAT-ED BY KNOWLEDGE RATHER THAN COMMODITIES.

# five

# Pensions — Personal Plans (RRSPs)

**5**

**T**axes are one of the greatest deterrents to achieving wealth accumulation; therefore, any method of sheltering an individual's income would be welcome. In 1957 the Government created an ideal shelter for Canadian taxpayers — the Registered Retirement Savings Plan (RRSP). The major benefits of RRSPs are:

**R**eap big rewards with years of TAX-FREE COMPOUNDING

**R**educe your TAXABLE INCOME and DEFER INCOME TAX

**S**helter your RETIREMENT SAVINGS GROWTH

**P**repare yourself for a FINANCIALLY SECURE RETIREMENT

The RRSP is a procedural investment tool that allows Canadians the opportunity to enjoy tax-sheltered compounding in order to amass a substantial pool of retirement capital. The income earned inside an RRSP is tax-deferred until removed at retirement by way of a cash withdrawal or payments from a Registered Retirement Income Fund (RRIF), Life Income Fund (LIF), or annuity. These maturity options are designed to allow a systematic flow of taxable income over the remainder of your lifetime.

The cornerstone of most successful retirement plans is an RRSP, or a company pension plan supplemented with an RRSP. RRSPs are easily the most widely used procedural tool for funding an individual's retirement beyond company and government pensions. Many types of RRSPs exist, but common to all is the fact that contributions are sheltered from current taxation.

## Who Can Invest in an RRSP?

An RRSP is a contract between you and the issuer and is approved by Government. All Canadian taxpayers, subject to an earned income test, may contribute to an RRSP until age 69. The main components of earned income are: net salary or wages, disability pension, CPP/QPP, net rental income, alimony or maintenance received, and certain royalties.

## Tax Shelters Provide an Extra Edge

Assume you are an investor in a 50% tax bracket and that you have $1,000 of income available for an investment offering a 12% return.

| | INVESTMENT (Unsheltered) | RRSP (Sheltered) |
|---|---|---|
| Earned Income $1,000 | $ 1,000 | $ 1,000 |
| Income Taxes (50%) | 500 | |
| Available for Investment | 500 | 1,000 |
| Compound @ 6% for 30 years | $41,900 | $270,290 |

As you can see, the $1,000 investment in the RRSP is compounding at 12%, and provides a six times greater return than the unsheltered investment after 30 years. The unsheltered funds available for investment each year are $500 after-tax and at 12% would produce $60 income the first year.

However, the income would also be taxable each year and assuming a 50% tax rate, the net effective compound rate of return would be 6% for the 30 years, or $41,900. Of course, the funds accumulated in the RRSP will become taxable as they are taken out at maturity. Even so, your investment will be worth over three times more, even after taxes, than the same investment outside an RRSP. And that is all due to years of tax-sheltered compounding.

**$1,000 Investment Sheltered vs. Unsheltered Compounding at 12%**

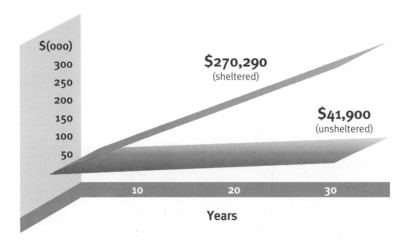

### Are You Getting Enough from Your RRSP?

The performance of your RRSP is very important to your financial success. For many Canadians, their RRSP is the only major tool they use to accumulate wealth, outside of owning their home.

Assume an annual contribution of $1,000 in each of the following savings and investment vehicles. A typical experience during the last thirty years might have been as follows:

## Savings and Investment Returns

| | Rate of Return | Dollars Compounded | Type of Specialty |
|---|---|---|---|
| **$1,000 Per Year Compounded Annually for 30 Years** | **16%** | $615,160 | **Precious Metals** <br> **Common Stock** <br>   - Aggressive / Specialty <br> **Mutual Funds** - Sector / Global / <br>   - 3rd World / International |
| | **14%** | $406,740 | **Common Stock** - Growth <br> **Mutual Funds** <br>   - Growth (CDN) / Growth (US) |
| | **12%** | $270,290 | **Common Stock** - Income <br> **Mutual Funds** <br>   - Balanced (Diversified) |
| | **10%** | $180,940 | **Convertible** - Preferreds <br> **Convertible** - Debentures & Bonds <br> **Preferreds** |
| | **8%** | $122,350 | **Mutual Funds** - Fixed Income <br> **Bonds & Debentures** <br> **Mortgages** |
| | **6%** | $83,800 | **Mutual Funds** - Bond/Mortgage <br> **GICs / TDs / CDs** |
| | **4%** | $58,330 | **Mutual Funds** - T-Bills <br> **CSBs / CTBs** <br> **Mutual Funds** - Money Market |
| | **2%** | $40,568 | **90-Day Deposits** <br> **Premium Savings** <br> **Daily Interest** |
| | **0%** | $30,000 | **Chequing / Savings** |

## RRSPs — A Formula For Financial Independence

Perhaps the greatest opportunity Canadians have is the ability to ensure their financial independence. Yet statistics have shown that less than 50% of Canadians participate in the annual rites of winter.

Our seminars and workshops are mainly sponsored by companies that have a higher end range of benefits including a corporate pension plan (RPP) for their employees.

We have solicited information in our seminars showing that over 80% of the participants have made RRSP contributions within the last few years. Therefore, the same people who are covered by a (RPP) are also topping up their RRSPs when they have additional contribution room.

Our conclusion: In the future there will be an even greater disparity between those who "have" and "have not".

## RRSPs — The Key to Your Financial Future!

- RRSPs are the cornerstone of most successful retirement plans.
- Most Canadians who wish to maintain their standard of living during retirement will need income from non-government plans such as RRSPs.
- Tax support for RRSPs and employer pensions is meant to encourage Canadians to supplement their government pensions.
- RRSPs can provide you with the peace of mind you'll need to enjoy a retirement that could span two or three decades.
- If you could only make one investment per year with a limited amount of money, the RRSP umbrella would probably be the best place for your funds.

The future belongs to those who **choose** knowledge-based skills and tools as their experiences. ■ The absolute edge in future work will belong to those who **invest** wisely in new experiences to increase their capabilities. ■ Every now and then it makes sense to go home and revisit where you came from and to **examine** the life you now live, in order to **determine** where you would like to go. ■ Leisure time is earned and, like money, it should be spent wisely and invested over the long-term in a rewarding life.

"He spent his health to get his wealth. And now he is spending his wealth to get back his health."

— Lloyd Percival

*IF YOU KNEW YOU WERE GOING TO DIE TOMORROW, YOU'D KNOW HOW TO LIVE TODAY.*

# six

# The Six
# Powers Of Success

**6**

**A**ll of our corporate seminars and workshops emphasize setting goals that require a balanced approach to successful financial and lifestyle planning. Many people have enjoyed tremendous financial success but at the expense of poor health and a breakdown in family and personal relationships.

1 PHYSICAL HEALTH          4 PERSONAL SKILLS

2 PRECIOUS RELATIONSHIPS   5 PERSONAL FULFILLMENT

3 PERSONAL CONTROL         6 PURSUIT OF FINANCIAL FREEDOM

What did Marilyn Monroe, Elvis Presley, Janis Joplin, Jimi Hendrix, Freddie Prinz, John Belushi, Mama Cass Elliott and John Candy have in common? They died relatively young, they were in the arts and entertainment industry, they enjoyed a lot of financial success, they all died of some form of substance abuse. The missing link in each of these lives was balance; these people all had success in the financial power, but were lacking in the other powers. Ordinarily, people will not come to an untimely or unlikely end if their life is in balance. Virtually everything in our lives when taken to extreme can harm us. The substance abuse that took the lives of Mama Cass Elliott and John Candy was food.

Probably the first and most important power to concentrate on is your physical health. If you haven't got your physical health, it doesn't matter what else is going on in your life because you'll find it difficult to enjoy if you're uncomfortable and in a lot of pain or discomfort.

The second most important power is precious relationships. Nothing in this life is more important than the relationships you have with family and friends. It is said that if you have even one or two really close friends in a lifetime, it is a major accomplishment.

Notice that we have placed the financial power in sixth place. Most people think that this is the most important power of all. While its importance cannot be denied, most people would not trade the financial power to the exclusion of a balance within the other five powers.

We refer to the financial power as the pursuit of financial freedom. Why? Because happiness is in the chase, the adventure. There are probably not too many of us who haven't thought that if we had been left a couple of million dollars by our parents or a wealthy relative, life's burdens would be a little easier. Well, perhaps that's true, but we know that historically, second or third generation wealth is often not a blessing to the person who receives it. Some people manage inherited wealth very well, but a large percentage of people experience problems because they didn't acquire the money themselves.

It's the same situation with lotteries such as Lotto 6/49. Many people buy a lottery ticket thinking that if they won a million or two it would change their lives for the better. Others realize that money isn't the answer to inner happiness. The instant gratification of a lottery windfall, while providing a lot of excitement, is not usually fulfilling.

Now that we have taken a quick look at three of the six powers of success, we see that a balanced lifestyle means we should strive to embrace all of the powers equally. We'll further assume that most people are going to acquire the financial power in life the old fashion way — diligently in pursuit of financial freedom. Therefore, it's time to turn our attention to the core subject matter of this handbook — financial planning.

## What Is Financial Planning?

In simple terms, financial planning is the process of gathering, understanding, and managing your financial resources in order to use them more effectively for your own future. Financial planning is necessary if you wish to satisfy your own and your family's needs now and retire in dignity when the time comes.

### Why The Need?

The message of the last few budgets was that the Canadian Government can no longer afford to support all of the people in the manner to which they have become accustomed. The bottom line is that there will continue to be high taxes and further reductions in social programs.

### Why Many Personal Financial Plans Fail?

Most plans fail for four major reasons; two are private or totally controllable by the individual, and two are public- or government-related and out of your direct control.

| PRIVATE ENEMIES | PUBLIC ENEMIES |
|---|---|
| 1. Procrastination | 1. Taxes |
| 2. Attitude | 2. Inflation |

These four enemies wreak more havoc on the retirement dreams of Canadian investors than any others. It is absolutely essential that you come to terms with these four issues. NOW!

**50% of Canadians have no retirement plans—**

neither a pension plan (RPP) with their

employer nor an RRSP.  ▲  | Procrastination |

is simply the lack of a clear vision about

get started!                    "The secret

what you want to do.  ▲  What is easy to do

                                    of success

is easy not to do!  ▲  If investing was easy

                                    is constancy

we would already be doing it.  ▲  Above all,

                                    of purpose"

remember that no | decision | is in fact a

                                    — Disraeli

decision.  ▲  Most people underachieve

COMMITMENT IS THE

because they just can't get started.  ▲  Try?

GREATEST GIFT YOU

There is no try ... there is only do and not do!

CAN GIVE YOURSELF!

As the Nike commercial states: Just do It!

# Private Enemy #1: Procrastination

**7**

**T**he greatest reason for people failing to achieve financial independence is procrastination. There are five key things that many Canadians don't do that get them into trouble:

**They DO NOT set financial goals**

**They DO NOT have a cash management system**

**They DO NOT pay themselves first**

**They DO NOT plan tax savings**

**They DO NOT plan for risk (unexpected events)**

## " They do not plan to fail — they simply fail to plan "

In matters of personal finance, procrastination reveals its true character — self-sabotage. The longer you wait to put money to work for yourself, the more money you will require when you eventually need it. Retirement income is seldom a concern when people are young. A house, car, travel, and perhaps a boat or cottage, enjoy higher positions of financial priority. Too often people reach age 55 or 60 and realize the paycheques will stop coming in a few years, and they have not adequately planned to meet their future expenses.

## Towers Perrin Survey

According to a recent study by Towers Perrin, working Canadians are looking at the future with rose-coloured glasses. They have a high degree of confidence that they will have enough money for a comfortable retirement, but in fact, they are doing very little to assure themselves of a retirement with financial dignity.

### Level of Confidence

Pension plan members and non-members alike are optimistic about their retirement income. A total of 76% of plan members and 67% of non-members are very or somewhat confident that they will have enough to live comfortably in retirement.

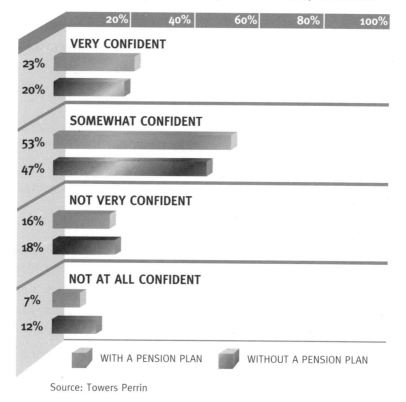

Source: Towers Perrin

## Primary Sources of Retirement Income

When asked to identify their number one source of retirement income, employees give top spot to either pension plans, if they are plan members — or personal savings, if they are non-members. All other potential sources — including government benefits — wind up far down the list.

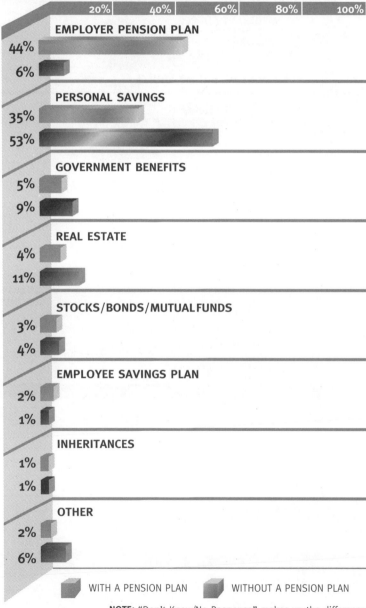

| | 20% | 40% | 60% | 80% | 100% |

**EMPLOYER PENSION PLAN**
44%
6%

**PERSONAL SAVINGS**
35%
53%

**GOVERNMENT BENEFITS**
5%
9%

**REAL ESTATE**
4%
11%

**STOCKS/BONDS/MUTUAL FUNDS**
3%
4%

**EMPLOYEE SAVINGS PLAN**
2%
1%

**INHERITANCES**
1%
1%

**OTHER**
2%
6%

WITH A PENSION PLAN    WITHOUT A PENSION PLAN

Source: Towers Perrin

**NOTE:** "Don't Know/No Response" makes up the difference between 100% and the percentage totals on some charts.

## Role of Personal Savings

A high percentage of employees rank personal savings as their first or second most important source of retirement income. Even 35% of pension plan members rank personal savings as number one.

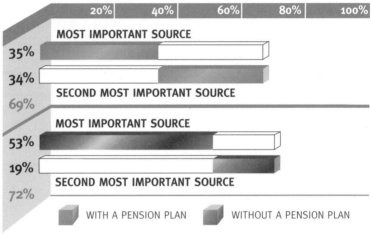

Source: Towers Perrin

## Too Little, Too Late

Although working Canadians recognize the importance of personal savings for their retirement, most appear to be procrastinating. However, by not saving enough earlier in their working lives, they are facing a formidable challenge in building sufficient retirement income.

For example, to accumulate $500,000, which will provide a lifetime pension of about $50,000 a year at age 65, this is how much an employee would have to save annually depending on the number of years until retirement. This assumes money is invested in monthly instalments at a 7% return.

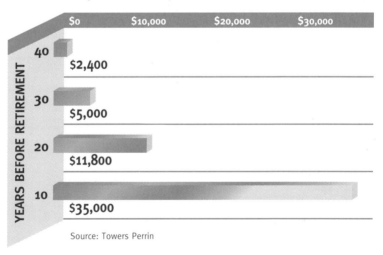

Source: Towers Perrin

## Amount of Annual Savings (Including Pension Plan Contributions)

Considering the importance employees place on savings and the fact that the following percentages include employee contributions to an employer-sponsored pension plan, the amount that working Canadians save is surprisingly small. It seems few are matching works with actions.

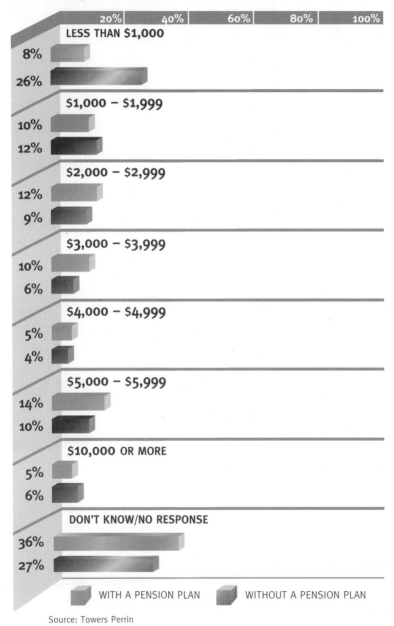

Source: Towers Perrin

## Pay Yourself First

The single most important concept to grasp is to **pay yourself first**. Many people come to the end of their working life wondering who really benefited from all their years of working. The government certainly got its share in taxes each year. The mortgage company got its share every month. Others who benefited were doctors, dentists, health care plans, insurance companies, auto dealers, and grocery stores. For most of us, not much remains for retirement savings after all the bills are paid. One sure way to avoid this all-too-common syndrome of "nothing left for me" is to **pay yourself first**.

Divide your work week into ten equal periods, two for each working day. Allocate your weekly take-home pay for Monday morning (10% of your total weekly take-home pay) to your savings program. Consider that every Monday, until noon, you are working for your own personal corporation. As that amount compounds year after working year, you'll guarantee that you won't end up at retirement wondering whose corporation your labour benefited. You'll know it was your own personal company!

**Pay Yourself First**

| | MONDAY | TUESDAY | WEDNESDAY | THURSDAY | FRIDAY |
|---|---|---|---|---|---|
| am $ | SAVINGS | | | OTHER | |
| pm | | TAXES | | MONTHLY BILLS | |

## The Corporate World Today

Rapidly disappearing are the formerly predictable 9:00 a.m. to 5:00 p.m. workdays for a single employer offering a paternalistic security blanket during one's career and post-retirement. Employees today must constantly train, retrain, enhance old skills, and add new ones in order to survive.

Job-hopping and career-hopping are quickly becoming the norm for employees, which necessitates a new reality and approach to their investments and the management of their pension plans. Many of us are far too dependent on our employers, but this does not fit the new reality. We must accept ownership of our pension plans, and the choices we make today will determine the pensions we receive tomorrow.

Prior to 1985, Canada had two borrowers for every saver. Now the situation has reversed with two savers for every borrower. The leading edge of the older boomer generation are starting to save ferociously for their retirements. The new reality has set in — governments and employers can't do it all. You can't afford to **procrastinate** another day.

"The remarkable thing is we have a **choice** every day, regarding the attitude we will embrace for that day. We cannot change our past... we cannot change the fact that people will act in a certain way. We cannot change the inevitable. The only thing we can do is play on the one string we have, and that is our attitude . I am convinced that life is 10% what happens to me and 90% how I react to it. And so it is with you...we are in **charge** of our attitudes."

—Charles Swindoll

"The journey of a thousand miles begins with a single step. You've already taken that step. The right attitude will keep you going towards your goal."
—Lao Tzu

"The worst bankrupt in the world is the man who has lost his enthusiasm. Let a man lose everything else in the world but his enthusiasm and he will come through again to success."
—H.W. Arnold

YOU ARE THE PRODUCT
OF WHAT YOU CHOOSE
FOR YOUR LIFE SITUATION.
YOU HAVE THE CAPACITY
TO MAKE HEALTHY "CHOICES"
FOR YOURSELF BY CHANGING
YOUR "ATTITUDE" TO ONE OF
"CREATIVE ALIVENESS."
THE LONGER YOU WAIT —
THE STEEPER THE CLIMB.

# eight

# Private Enemy #2: Attitude

**8**

**M**uch has been written about positive mental attitude. Hundreds of books and courses and a host of inspirational seminars offer encouragement to help people recharge their batteries. Maintaining a positive mental attitude in today's world is not easy. Our environment seems to support negativity. Most of what we read and watch in newspapers and on television is filled with negative input — natural disasters, fire, rape, murder, famine, war, international tension, lawsuits, divorce, and more. If the majority of your input is negative, the output will be as well, because the mind processes thoughts like a computer. We are bombarded by negative information because negativity sells — but sells what? Remember:

**A Bad Attitude Produces Bad Results.**
**A Fair Attitude Produces Fair Results.**
**A Good Attitude Produces Good Results.**
**Success breeds success; failure breeds failure.**

Let's examine success, the result of a positive "I Can" attitude.

An "I Can" attitude sets a positive cycle in motion. Your faith and belief system programs the mental attitude of a winner. You do what you have to do to succeed. You can be successful;

you can have positive results. This leads you to take great leaps forward, which, in turn, breeds still more positive results. Developing a positive mental attitude can carry you beyond the vicious circle of negativity to the victory circle. It is easy to write about and more difficult to put into practice, but it is inevitably more rewarding.

**The Laws of Attitude**

## Success — From Concept to Action

Success comes when you put yourself on the line. Positive mental attitude is the key. The time to start planning for a comfortable retirement is now. Yesterday is gone. Tomorrow is a result of what we think and do today. Start now!

**Winners never quit! Quitters never win!**

## Your Career Attitude

Add value to your career. Contribute more than just time. It's your value-added contribution that counts. Many employees work hard and stay busy, but add very little real value. They mistakenly think they should be paid for putting in time, but time is only the measurement used to assess value. Employers will almost always pay for value and your security depends on how valuable you are to the organization.

## Corporate Survival Tools for the 21st Century

The major issue is employability versus employment.

- No employer has an obligation to employ you.
- You can take action to make yourself employable.
- By upgrading skills, employees have a much better chance of finding work in the Information Age economy.
- Many jobs in the future will be based on 3-month to 3-year contracts.
- Traditional training, skills enhancement, and higher education don't guarantee employment, but they are a prerequisite to making an individual employable.
- Sooner or later you're going to arrive — the question is where?

Now is the time to plan the next five years. Ask yourself, how valuable can I become?

## The Education Connection

Since 1990 there has been a net increase of more than 400,000 jobs across Canada, virtually all of them requiring some post-secondary education.

| Level of education | Change in number of people employed, 1990-94 |
|---|---|
| Grade 8 or less | - 147,000 |
| Some high school | - 373,000 |
| High-school graduate | - 158,000 |
| Some post-secondary | + 43,000 |
| College or technical degree | + 646,000 |
| University graduate | + 452,000 |

Source: Statistics Canada

## Your Attitude Equals Your Results

You are in control of your destiny and only *you* can make the decisions that affect your life and your finances. *You* are where the buck stops — and the dollars begin.

Canadians have endured two decades of tax,

borrow, and spend governments ● Its time to

Most families have two breadwinners

pay the piper! As you age you have less

DURING THE NEXT

working 40 hours per week and yet

energy to earn income; therefore, you must

24 HOURS, THE

real family income has fallen during

create a wealth system during your working

GOVERNMENT WILL

the last decade.

years to support you in your retirement years.

SPEND IN EXCESS OF

● Money is always at work 24 hours

$82 MILLION AND

per day and never takes a rest, so choose

THE SAME FOR EVERY

your investments carefully. ● The primary

24-HOUR PERIOD

payment during your working career

AFTER THAT.

should be made to yourself to ensure ade-

quate financial reserves for your retirement.

# nine

# Public Enemy #1:
## Taxes

**9**

**S**ome close their eyes to taxes, some plug their ears, and some shut their mouths, but everyone pays through the nose. The trick is to keep what is really yours.

### Why a Tax on Income?

Our Government provides us with many services. All require great expenditures of money. This money is raised primarily through taxation.

When the government spends more money than it brings in, it is said to have a deficit. But, unlike a business or an individual, if the government does not have enough money, it just prints up more paper dollars. This is one of the major causes of inflation. So, with things costing more and more each year, the government has to collect more dollars or print more money. It is a no-win situation — higher taxes or higher inflation.

### Two Methods of Taxation

There are two methods of levying income tax. The first is on one's ability to pay. The second is calculated on benefits received.

Our system today is called a progressive tax system. The more an individual earns, the larger percentage of income goes to income tax. In other words, the more your make, the more they take.

## Personal Tax Rates

The Canadian tax system has three basic tax brackets. Your applicable marginal tax rate increases as your taxable income increases; your marginal tax rate is the rate of tax you pay on each additional dollar of income earned. Marginal tax rates show the combined federal tax rate for each bracket including surtaxes and a provincial rate of 58% of the amount of federal tax payable, based on an average of all provincial tax rates.

**Marginal Tax Rates**

| Taxable Income | Federal Rate | Combined Federal/ Provincial Rate* | Combined Federal/ Provincial Rate Including Surtaxes |
|---|---|---|---|
| $0 – $29,590 | 17% | 27% | 27% |
| $29,591 – $59,180 | 26% | 41% | 45% |
| $59,181 + | 29% | 46% | 53% |

*Assumes a provincial tax of 58% of the Federal rate.

## Three Types of Investment Income — Interest, Dividends, and Capital Gains

There are three basic forms of investment income: interest, dividends, and capital gains. Each type of income is treated differently for tax purposes. Therefore, it is more important for the investor to focus on an investment's after-tax return rather than the pre-tax return.

**Taxation of Investment Income**

| | |
|---|---|
| Interest and Foreign Income | 100% fully taxed |
| Dividends | 25% gross up and 13.3% tax credit |
| Capital Gains | first 25% of gain tax-free; 75% taxable on the balance |

## The After-Tax Retention Per $1,000

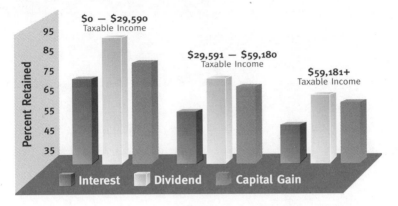

## Personal Tax Management Strategies and Tactics

There are three main ways to reduce your taxes:

1. **Reduce Your Taxable Income:** For example, you could borrow for investment and pay down your mortgage.
2. **Reduce Your Effective Tax Rate:** For example, adjust your portfolio so that you receive more dividend income than interest income; establish an education trust for your children or a spousal RRSP for income splitting.
3. **Defer Taxable Income to Future Years:** Unrealized capital gains defer taxes until the asset is sold. An RRSP defers taxes until retirement. In effect, you have an interest-free loan from the government.

Broken down into their specifics, these three approaches create over 100 different tax-reducing tactics, but that is the subject of another book. The three approaches do, however, produce two fundamental tax-saving strategies:

1. Your number one strategy should be to save and invest.
2. Your number two strategy should be to complement your number one strategy with tax savings and tax deferral strategies.

**Every** employee has the potential

to have a very comfortable retirement for

the first five to ten years . The concern is

whether they can continue to maintain a

comfortable lifestyle for the next five,

ten, fifteen, or more years because of the

ravages of taxflation . Above all, remember

that inflation is **not** an increase in prices,

although prices do increase. It is a decrease

Taxflation

in the value of your money. In retirement,

one or both partners will likely see prices

triple or quadruple prior to their demise.

# ten

# Public Enemy #2: Inflation

**10**

**W**hat is a dollar? We all know what a dollar is worth today in terms of what it will buy in goods and services. But what will our dollar buy in goods or services in 10 or 20 years if inflation averages 5% per year? In just 20 years, the purchasing power of a dollar today would decline to just $0.38.

| | | $1.00 | .61 | .38 |
|---|---|---|---|---|
| 1977 | 1987 | 1997 | 2007 | 2017 |

Look at what has happened to prices on these products over a period of 30 years.

| | 1966 | 1996 |
|---|---|---|
| Margarine (kilogram) | $ 0.77 | $ 4.99 |
| Ground Beef (kilogram) | 1.74 | 5.49 |
| Milk (1 litre) | 0.35 | 1.69 |
| Cotton Dress Shirt | 7.00 | 45.00 |
| Regular Gas (1 litre) | 0.11 | 0.57 |
| Passenger Car (N.A. average) | 4,500.00 | 20,409.00 |

You can see what the ravages of inflation in our economy can do to the future purchasing power of the dollar. A dollar is only worth a dollar at a specific point in time. In 10, 20, and 30 years from now, assuming the following base prices for 1996, what might these same products cost you if inflation were to average 5%?

| | 1996 | 2006 | 2016 | 2026 |
|---|---|---|---|---|
| Margarine (kilogram) | $ 4.99 | $ 8.13 | $ 13.22 | $ 21.56 |
| Ground Beef (kilogram) | 5.49 | 8.95 | 14.59 | 23.72 |
| Milk (1 litre) | 1.69 | 2.75 | 4.48 | 7.30 |
| Cotton Dress Shirt | 45.00 | 73.35 | 119.25 | 194.40 |
| Regular Gas (1 litre) | 0.57 | 0.93 | 1.51 | 2.46 |
| Passenger Car (N.A. average) | 20,409.00 | 33,267.00 | 54,084.00 | 88,167.00 |

Consumer prices have increased dramatically over the past few decades. This constant inflationary trend has already eaten away 70% of the dollar's value over the past 20 years. It is not unreasonable to assume that inflation will continue averaging somewhere between 4% and 5% over the long term.

**Canada's Inflation Rate History**

| | Average Annual Compound Inflation Rates | |
|---|---|---|
| | Number of Years | Inflation Rate |
| 1991 – '95 | 5 | 2.0% |
| 1986 – '95 | 10 | 3.3 |
| 1981 – '95 | 15 | 4.6 |
| 1976 – '95 | 20 | 5.8 |
| 1971 – '95 | 25 | 6.0 |
| 1970 – '79 | 10 | 7.4 |
| 1970 – '84 | 15 | 7.9 |
| 1950 – '95 | 46 | 4.4 |

## How Much Money Will You Need At Retirement?

Imagine you have accumulated $1,000,000 by the time you retire. How much after-tax income will your $1,000,000 capital generate. Assuming a 10% pre-tax return, the after-tax amount would generate about $50,000 per year.

That's great for year one, but if you were to live for 20 years in retirement and inflation were to average 5%, the purchasing power of each dollar would decline to $0.38.

## Compound Discount Table for $1.00

Annual Rate of Return

| Year | 1% | 3% | 5% | 7% | 9% | 11% | 13% | 15% |
|------|------|------|------|------|------|------|------|------|
| 1 | 0.99 | 0.97 | 0.95 | 0.93 | 0.92 | 0.90 | 0.88 | 0.87 |
| 2 | 0.98 | 0.94 | 0.91 | 0.87 | 0.84 | 0.81 | 0.78 | 0.76 |
| 3 | 0.97 | 0.92 | 0.86 | 0.82 | 0.77 | 0.73 | 0.69 | 0.66 |
| 4 | 0.96 | 0.89 | 0.82 | 0.76 | 0.71 | 0.66 | 0.61 | 0.57 |
| 5 | 0.95 | 0.86 | 0.78 | 0.71 | 0.65 | 0.59 | 0.54 | 0.50 |
| 6 | 0.94 | 0.84 | 0.75 | 0.67 | 0.60 | 0.53 | 0.48 | 0.43 |
| 7 | 0.93 | 0.81 | 0.71 | 0.62 | 0.55 | 0.48 | 0.43 | 0.38 |
| 8 | 0.92 | 0.79 | 0.68 | 0.58 | 0.50 | 0.43 | 0.38 | 0.33 |
| 9 | 0.91 | 0.77 | 0.64 | 0.54 | 0.46 | 0.39 | 0.33 | 0.28 |
| 10 | 0.91 | 0.74 | 0.61 | 0.51 | 0.42 | 0.35 | 0.29 | 0.25 |
| 11 | 0.90 | 0.72 | 0.58 | 0.48 | 0.39 | 0.32 | 0.26 | 0.21 |
| 12 | 0.89 | 0.70 | 0.56 | 0.44 | 0.36 | 0.29 | 0.23 | 0.19 |
| 13 | 0.88 | 0.68 | 0.53 | 0.41 | 0.33 | 0.26 | 0.20 | 0.16 |
| 14 | 0.87 | 0.66 | 0.51 | 0.39 | 0.30 | 0.23 | 0.18 | 0.14 |
| 15 | 0.86 | 0.64 | 0.48 | 0.36 | 0.27 | 0.21 | 0.16 | 0.12 |
| 16 | 0.85 | 0.62 | 0.46 | 0.34 | 0.25 | 0.19 | 0.14 | 0.11 |
| 17 | 0.84 | 0.61 | 0.44 | 0.32 | 0.23 | 0.17 | 0.13 | 0.09 |
| 18 | 0.84 | 0.59 | 0.42 | 0.30 | 0.21 | 0.15 | 0.11 | 0.08 |
| 19 | 0.83 | 0.57 | 0.40 | 0.28 | 0.19 | 0.14 | 0.10 | 0.07 |
| 20 | 0.82 | 0.55 | 0.38 | 0.26 | 0.18 | 0.12 | 0.09 | 0.06 |
| 21 | 0.81 | 0.54 | 0.36 | 0.24 | 0.16 | 0.11 | 0.08 | 0.05 |
| 22 | 0.80 | 0.52 | 0.34 | 0.23 | 0.15 | 0.10 | 0.07 | 0.05 |
| 23 | 0.80 | 0.51 | 0.33 | 0.21 | 0.14 | 0.09 | 0.06 | 0.04 |
| 24 | 0.79 | 0.49 | 0.31 | 0.20 | 0.13 | 0.08 | 0.05 | 0.03 |
| 25 | 0.78 | 0.48 | 0.30 | 0.18 | 0.12 | 0.07 | 0.05 | 0.03 |
| 30 | 0.74 | 0.41 | 0.23 | 0.13 | 0.08 | 0.04 | 0.03 | 0.02 |
| 35 | 0.71 | 0.36 | 0.18 | 0.09 | 0.05 | 0.03 | 0.01 | 0.01 |
| 40 | 0.67 | 0.31 | 0.14 | 0.07 | 0.03 | 0.02 | 0.01 | 0 00 |

Let's further imagine that you retire in 1997. Now you have the time to pursue recreation, hobbies, crafts, sports, and maybe even time to write a letter to an old friend. How much does it cost to mail a letter in 1997 compared to 25 years ago? .45¢ versus .08¢ in 1972.

## Canadian Stamps — Purchasing Power

| 1972 .08¢ | 1997 .45¢ | 2022 (?) |
|-----------|-----------|----------|

As you can see the inflation increase over the last 25 years was 563%. More important, what will it cost to mail a letter 25 years from now? And what asset allocation strategy is necessary to maintain the purchasing power of your dollar? Too many people overlook the effect of inflation in their planning and the fact that inflation packs a double wallop at retirement — not only will your capital generate less income, but your expenses will increase each year with inflation.

## Taxflation—The Real Story on Purchasing Power

Would you like to know the investment return required to maintain the purchasing power of your money under various inflation and tax rates? First let's review the three major tax brackets.

**Combined Federal and Provincial Tax Rate\* Including Surtaxes**

| | |
|---|---|
| $0 − $29,590 | = 27% |
| $29,591 − $59,180 | = 45% |
| $59,181 and up | = 53% |

\* Assumes a Provincial Tax of 58% of the Federal Rate

Now let's combine these tax brackets with various inflation rates to introduce the concept of **taxflation**.

## Taxflation

Investment returns needed to maintain the purchasing power of your money:

| | Projected Rate of Inflation % | | | | | |
|---|---|---|---|---|---|---|
| Tax Bracket | 3% | 4% | 5% | 6% | 7% | 8% |
| 25% | 4.0 | 5.3 | 6.6 | 8.0 | 9.3 | 10.7 |
| 30 | 4.3 | 5.7 | 7.1 | 8.6 | 10.1 | 11.4 |
| 35 | 4.6 | 6.2 | 7.7 | 9.2 | 10.8 | 12.3 |
| 40 | 5.0 | 6.6 | 8.3 | 10.0 | 11.7 | 13.3 |
| 45 | 5.5 | 7.2 | 9.1 | 10.9 | 12.7 | 14.5 |
| 50 | 6.0 | 8.0 | 10.0 | 12.0 | 14.0 | 16.0 |

Here's how it works. Assume you are in a 45% tax bracket and inflation is projected to average 5%. You would have to earn 9.1% on a taxable investment just to maintain the purchasing power of your dollars. (Find 45% tax bracket and 5% inflation where these two lines intersect = 9.1%).

Now ask yourself "Are any of my investments currently earning less than the break-even point in this example?"

If your answer to this question is "Yes," then there is a real message for you to capture in this exercise — understanding the difference between saving and investing. Savings could lead to a concept called "going broke safely," while investing can provide a strategy to achieve higher rates of return (with calculated risks) through asset allocation and investment diversification.

## Inflation Summary

Seriously consider the following investment recommendation. This investment was selling for $100 in 1951. By 1961, it's value dropped to $88; by 1971, it was worth $63; by 1981, it was worth $28; and by 1991 it was just $18. It is projected to be worth about $13 in 2001. Before you say, "You've got to be kidding," you should know that this investment is recommended every day by our government, our banks, our trust companies, and our other deposit-taking institutions.

What is this investment? The Canadian dollar. Every time you purchase a savings vehicle, based on the value of the dollar, you risk losing real purchasing power in the long run, due to the ravages of inflation. Still feel like saving your money? Still feel like-turning a blind eye to taxes and inflation? Still feel like going broke?

# Invest,
# invest!

saving as fast as they can and still fear it won't be enough. ◆ Their energy would be better spent on learning the laws of compounding. ◆ None of the great invest-ment money managers ever gets caught up in short-term thinking. ◆ They never evaluate their performance over the short-term. ◆ They stick with their managerial style and believe in the process; that time will eventually win out. ◆ You can only have two things in life — reasons or results. ◆ Reasons don't count.

"I don't know what the Seven Wonders of the World are but I know what the Eighth Wonder is: Compound Interest."
— Baron Rothschild

"We must use time creatively — and forever realize that time is always hope to do great things."
— Martin Luther King Jr.

"Money makes money, and the money that money makes makes more money."
— Benjamin Franklin

# eleven

# Time, Money, And Compounding

**11**

# Time is the best friend you have.

Imagine you recently turned age 52. If the average life expectancy is mid-70s for a male, how many years are you expected to have left? Twenty-three years. Now, while we don't like to put a number on one's lifespan, how many weeks do you have left assuming you live to age 75? 1196! Let's suppose you spend this week to no good purpose then you'll only have 1195 weeks left. And if you waste next week as well, you'll be down to an inventory of 1194 weeks. When you start to think of your life in terms of weeks, rather than years, you begin to realize how precious time is. This realization can be almost frightening and yet when the energy of time is harnessed, you can bring it under your control and make it work for you.

Time affects every dimension of your life, including leisure, wellness, resources, relationships, and finances. Probably the most important aspect of time applies to ones financial well-being. When is the best time to start planning for retirement? Ideally, the day you enter the workforce. It takes a minimum of 20 years and often 30 to 35 years to build the assets most people will need in order to enjoy their retirement without major financial sacrifices. And obviously, if you plan to take an early leave in your mid to late 50s, you will need an exceptionally good plan because you will have fewer years to achieve your financial security.

You'll need to achieve quantum leaps with your investment portfolio performance to have any hope of retiring sooner rather than later. You can no longer take a passive approach to your investing. You need a clear understanding of time and how it relates to different investments. Consider the performance of the following assets during the last 45 years.

**Best Performing Assets January 1, 1950 - June 30, 1996**

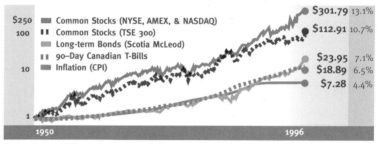

Source: Di Meo, Anthony & Dexter Robinson, ANDEX Chart for Canadian Investors, 1996, ANDEX Associates, Windsor, Ontario.

Now that we have looked at time as it pertains to your lifespan and your financial considerations, let's examine the concept of your personal financial planning factory.

There are only two raw materials that can ever be placed in your factory — money and time. How you manage, manipulate, and massage these two ingredients will determine the output from your factory. We call this output comfortable retirement and it can begin at any age you want, dependent upon how well you manage the two inputs of time and money.

Based on your personal time frames, you will ideally design your asset allocation to deliver the retirement outcome you would like to achieve.

Another aspect of time is to have a clear understanding of investment planning time frames as they pertain to your needs.

**Investment Planning Time Frames**

| | |
|---|---|
| When planning for 1 year | — Cash Reserves |
| When planning for 2 years | — Fixed Income (Bonds) |
| When planning for 3 to 5 years | — Balanced/Diversified |
| When planning for 6 to 10 years | — Equity |
| When planning for a lifetime | — KNOWLEDGE |

## The Effect of Time on Compounding

Many Canadians consistently underestimate the impact of an extra 1% or 2% annual compounding over time. This often leads to choosing so-called safe investments such as traditional bank and trust savings accounts, guaranteed investment certificates (GICs), term deposits (TDs), and Canada Savings Bonds (CSBs). The long-term result for these investors is that they go broke safely. Mind you it feels good in the process.

## A Short Lesson on Compounding

Most people don't really understand the concept of compounding. If they did, they would be obtaining much better investment results. So how does compounding really work?

**Compound Interest**

| | Capital | Rate | Interest | Total |
|---|---|---|---|---|
| Year 1 | $1000 | 10% | = $100 | $1100 |
| Year 2 | $1100 | 10% | = $110 | $1210 |
| Year 3 | $1210 | 10% | = $121 | $1331 |

It's hard to get excited about a three-year compounding cycle starting with $1,000 and ending up with $1,331. And this is why many Canadians never grasp the true potential of the long-term effects of compounding. In fact most make all of their decisions based on one year at a time. Their rationale works like this. Assume the following investments are currently yielding these returns:

| | |
|---|---|
| Chequing/Savings Account | .25% |
| Premium Savings Account | 2.00% |
| Canadian Treasury Bills | 3.05% |
| Term Deposit: 1-Year | 3.20% |
| Guaranteed Investment Certificate: 5-year | 5.00% |
| Stock Market (guesstimate) | 10.50% |

Most investors look at the so-called guaranteed riskless returns of the term deposit at 3.2% instead of the stock market's much riskier long-term potential of 10.5%. They believe that to forego the difference of a 7.3% return for the sure bet that the term deposit will produce, a 3.2% return is a smart choice. And it's guaranteed by the Canadian Deposit Insurance Corporation (CDIC), which also makes good common sense. And they are absolutely right if their time frame is only one year. But if we are talking about a "rest of your life" plan, perhaps spanning 30 or 40 years, you need to understand what long-term compounding can do for you.

Let's take a look at the **Future Value of $1** table and compute the returns for three different investors over the next 30 years. The first investor settles for a very conservative return of 4% in his/her factory over the 30 years and every $1 grows to $3.24. A second investor works his/her factory a little harder and manages a return of 8% for 30 years and produces $10.06 for the same $1 invested. A third investor takes a much more aggressive approach and by actively managing, manipulating, and massaging the investments each $1 invested delivers a 12% return and grows to $29.96. Three factories with the same $1 investment, give three very different results. What would you like the long-term compounding result to be in your factory?

## Future Value Of $1.00 Compounded Annually Beginning Of Year

Annual Rate of Return

| Year | 2% | 4% | 6% | 8% | 10% | 12% | 14% | 16% |
|------|------|------|-------|-------|-------|-------|--------|--------|
| 1 | 1.02 | 1.04 | 1.06 | 1.08 | 1.10 | 1.12 | 1.14 | 1.10 |
| 2 | 1.04 | 1.08 | 1.12 | 1.17 | 1.21 | 1.25 | 1.30 | 1.35 |
| 3 | 1.06 | 1.12 | 1.19 | 1.26 | 1.33 | 1.40 | 1.48 | 1.56 |
| 4 | 1.08 | 1.17 | 1.26 | 1.36 | 1.46 | 1.57 | 1.69 | 1.81 |
| 5 | 1.10 | 1.22 | 1.34 | 1.47 | 1.61 | 1.76 | 1.93 | 2.10 |
| 6 | 1.13 | 1.27 | 1.42 | 1.59 | 1.77 | 1.97 | 2.19 | 2.44 |
| 7 | 1.15 | 1.32 | 1.50 | 1.71 | 1.95 | 2.21 | 2.50 | 2.83 |
| 8 | 1.17 | 1.37 | 1.59 | 1.85 | 2.14 | 2.48 | 2.85 | 3.28 |
| 9 | 1.20 | 1.42 | 1.69 | 2.00 | 2.36 | 2.77 | 3.25 | 3.80 |
| 10 | 1.22 | 1.48 | 1.79 | 2.16 | 2.59 | 3.11 | 3.71 | 4.41 |
| 11 | 1.24 | 1.54 | 1.90 | 2.33 | 2.85 | 3.48 | 4.23 | 5.12 |
| 12 | 1.27 | 1.60 | 2.01 | 2.52 | 3.14 | 3.90 | 4.82 | 5.94 |
| 13 | 1.29 | 1.67 | 2.13 | 2.72 | 3.45 | 4.36 | 5.49 | 6.89 |
| 14 | 1.32 | 1.73 | 2.26 | 2.94 | 3.80 | 4.89 | 6.26 | 7.99 |
| 15 | 1.35 | 1.80 | 2.40 | 3.17 | 4.18 | 5.47 | 7.14 | 9.27 |
| 16 | 1.37 | 1.87 | 2.54 | 3.43 | 4.59 | 6.13 | 8.14 | 10.75 |
| 17 | 1.40 | 1.95 | 2.69 | 3.70 | 5.05 | 6.87 | 9.28 | 12.47 |
| 18 | 1.43 | 2.03 | 2.85 | 4.00 | 5.56 | 7.69 | 10.58 | 14.46 |
| 19 | 1.46 | 2.11 | 3.03 | 4.32 | 6.12 | 8.61 | 12.06 | 16.78 |
| 20 | 1.49 | 2.19 | 3.21 | 4.66 | 6.73 | 9.65 | 13.74 | 19.46 |
| 21 | 1.52 | 2.28 | 3.40 | 5.03 | 7.40 | 10.80 | 15.67 | 22.57 |
| 22 | 1.55 | 2.37 | 3.60 | 5.44 | 8.14 | 12.10 | 17.86 | 26.19 |
| 23 | 1.58 | 2.46 | 3.82 | 5.87 | 8.95 | 13.55 | 20.36 | 30.38 |
| 24 | 1.61 | 2.56 | 4.05 | 6.34 | 9.85 | 15.18 | 23.21 | 35.24 |
| 25 | 1.64 | 2.67 | 4.29 | 6.85 | 10.83 | 17.00 | 26.46 | 40.87 |
| 30 | 1.81 | 3.24 | 5.74 | 10.06 | 17.45 | 29.96 | 50.95 | 85.85 |
| 35 | 2.00 | 3.95 | 7.69 | 14.79 | 28.10 | 52.80 | 98.10 | 180.31 |
| 40 | 2.21 | 4.80 | 10.29 | 21.72 | 45.26 | 93.05 | 188.88 | 378.72 |

## Where Are You On Your Lifeline?

There are three types of time:

**Past Time:** It's dead, we can't recapture it, we can't have it back, and it has no value.

**Future Time:** It has not been born yet, we can't use it, it hasn't arrived, and it has no value until it arrives.

**Present Time:** It's arrived, it's the here and now, and it has value.

| Learn | Earn | Yearn |
|-------|------|-------|
| BIRTH  **25** | **45** | **65**  DEATH |

What age are you now? At what age do you plan to retire?
Is time running out on your dream? What can you do to gain control of your future?

You may be in the early or latter stages of your working career. You are the best judge of where you are on your life-line and the amount of time you have to reach your goals. One of the recurring evaluation issues in every seminar or workshop we deliver is "I wish I'd attended this program ten or fifteen years ago!" The mindset behind this statement is "it's too late for me." Well, it's never too late!

Many investors in their late 40s or early 50s often feel that time has passed them by, however, with the right knowledge and encouragement, they can still take serious steps towards their retirement plans. The following table illustrates what's possible for an investment of $1200 per year starting at age 50. As you can see, the results 30 years later are very different, depending upon the rate of return achieved — almost six times greater at 14% versus 6%. Now visualize the result investing $300, $500, or several hundred per month for varying time frames between 20 and 30 years and at various rates of return, and you will see that there are all kinds of possibilities to build assets for your retirement even if you're already age 50.

### Future Value of $1,200 Invested at the Beginning of Each Year With Interest Compounded Monthly

| Age | Years Invested | Amount Invested | 6% | 10% | 14% |
|-----|---------------|-----------------|------|-------|-------|
| 50 | — | — | — | — | — |
| 60 | 10 | $12,000 | $ 16,920 | $ 21,612 | $ 27,912 |
| 70 | 20 | 24,000 | 47,724 | 80,112 | 140,196 |
| 80 | 30 | 36,000 | 103,752 | 238,476 | 591,840 |

Before we leave time, money, and compounding, let's look at one other tool called the "Rule of 72".

## The Rule of 72: Doubling Your Money

The "Rule of 72" is a handy tool you can use to measure the growth of your investments. Simply divide the number 72 by the annual rate of return, and the resulting figure will always equal the number of years it takes for money to double.

From the chart below, you can see that if you were earning a 6% rate of return on a $1,000 investment, and you divide that rate into 72, your money would double in 12 years (72 ÷ 6 = 12). The time frame for the investment is 24 years, therefore the $1,000 will double twice during this period to a total of $4,000.

A return of 15% would double your money in 72 ÷ 15 = 4.8 years. With $1,000 invested over 24 years, your investment would double five times to a total of $32,000.

**How $1,000 Grows Over a 24-Year Period at Various Rates of Return**

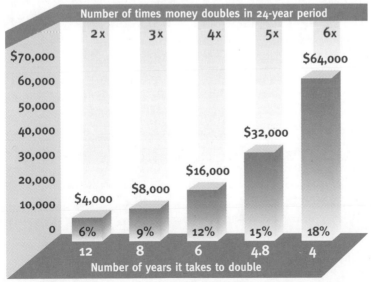

During the last 100 years, there have been

25 **bear** market slums (normal correc-

tions from the previous **bull** market

advance), and every single time the market

recovered and ultimately soared into new

high ground. ● From August 1982 to August

1987, the stock market **climbed** 250% and

then on October 19, 1987, the market

declined a record breaking 24% in one day.

IN CHINESE, THE WORD CRISIS IS COMPOSED OF TWO CHARACTERS.

● Every extreme in the stock market is

THE FIRST — THE SYMBOL OF DANGER;

answered with another extreme. ● Over the

THE SECOND — OPPORTUNITY.

long haul, sanity **always prevails!**

# twelve

## Cycles —
## The Investment Market Forces

**12**

**T**he price of anything can go up or down
in response to one or more of three elements only:

■ the demand for the product or service
■ the supply of the product or service
■ the value of the dollar

The first rule for investment success is based on the economic
law of demand and supply:

■ when demand increases, supply decreases and markets move up
■ when demand decreases, supply increases and markets move down

### So What Moves the Market?

The force of the market involves three key areas. The percentages
are an estimate of the amount of influence each area has in moving the market in a given direction:

**1** Investor Psychology — 50%
confidence, emotion — the "herd instinct"

**2** Technical — 30%
economy, industry position, popularity, and fad

**3** Hard Facts — 20%
earnings per share, dividends, return on investment, and selectivity

In addition to the law of supply and demand, and the changing value of the dollar (important to foreign investors), you need to understand that the stock market is a continuous cycle of peaks and troughs, mostly influenced by investor psychology, regarding the current market level in the cycle at any point in time.

Everything in life involves a cycle, beginning with life itself. The reproduction cycle passes from generation to generation. The four seasons, winter, spring, summer, and fall, are a cycle. Witness the changing of the tides influenced by the position of the moon and the earth as it revolves around the sun bringing us day and night. The stock market runs on cycles as well. There is a business cycle, an economic cycle, a presidential election cycle, a goods and services cycle, and a retail marketing cycle, to name a few. All of these cycles cause the stock market to fluctuate.

More zeal and energy, more fanatical hope, and more intense anguish have been extended over the past century in efforts to forecast the stock market than in almost any other single line of human action. Adam Smith, in *The Money Game*, stated, "You have to know what time of market it is."

Investment markets go in cycles like all the other rhythms of life. There are four basic cyclic phases:
■ Bottom Accumulation Bull Phase
■ Top Distribution/Bull Phase
■ Top Distribution/Bear Phase
■ Advanced Bear Phase Approaching Termination.

## Investment Cycle

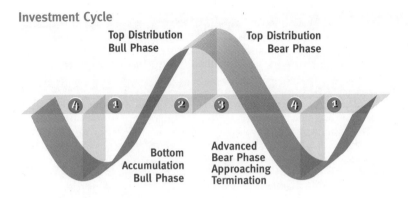

Top Distribution
Bull Phase

Top Distribution
Bear Phase

Bottom
Accumulation
Bull Phase

Advanced
Bear Phase
Approaching
Termination

## A Typical Cycle of Investor Emotions

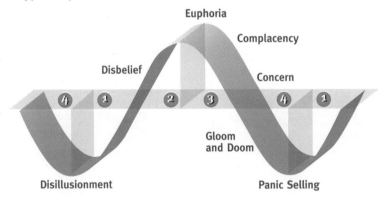

Euphoria

Complacency

Disbelief

Concern

Gloom
and Doom

Disillusionment

Panic Selling

## Types of Risk

The greatest influence on bond and stock market cycles is the impact of interest rates. In general, when interest rates are moving up, bond and stock markets move lower and vice versa. The impact of interest rate moves on the bond market is immediate and fairly precise. The stock market is also affected by the movement of interest rates as well as numerous other factors.

Successful financial planning involves taking some measured degree of risk and, in general, as you increase your degree of risk, you increase your potential reward. The types of risk are:

## Interest Rate Risk

As interest rates rise, the market value of fixed-return investments will, in most cases, decrease. This is interest rate risk. Since the relationship of price to interest rates is always **inverse,** we could think of falling rates as interest rate **opportunity.**

## Market Risk

The uncertainty in future prices that arises from changes in investor attitudes or other unknown factors is market risk. This involves a change in market psychology that may cause a security's price to decline regardless of any fundamental changes affecting the company's earning power.

## Purchasing Power (Inflation) Risk

This is a rise in prices that reduces the buying power of income and principal, or the chance that the value of your investment will deteriorate relative to a price index.

## Financial Risk

A financial or business risk occurs when there is some doubt about whether you will be able to collect future returns from an investment due to poor management, unfavourable economic conditions, increased competition, or outdated technology.

## Political Risk

Wage price controls, tax increases, changes in tariff and subsidy policies, government instability, nationalization of industry, dividend tax credits, and capital gains, are all political risks. All can easily depress investment values.

## Liquidity Risk

Liquidity risk is the danger that you will not be able to sell your investment without significant delays or costly penalties.

## Degrees of Risk

There is no such thing as a riskless investment. There are only degrees and types of risk. Fixed income investments such as CSBs, T-Bills, GICs, and bonds are subject to purchasing power risk as well as interest rate risk, both of which can be greater than the market risk involved in a well-balanced portfolio or a professionally managed equity fund.

Your degrees of risk can vary greatly. Many people think that by saving in a bank or trust company, by purchasing GICs, Term Deposits, or fixed income vehicles, they are completely safe. In reality, you're actually "going broke safely" by losing ground to inflation. If you were earning 5% on a Term Deposit and you were in a 40% tax bracket, you would have a net return of (5% - 2%) = 3% on an after-tax basis. If inflation were at 4.2%, you could be losing 1.2% on your capital or purchasing power!

While there is no risk to your original capital in this example, you have no real gains; you have merely lost purchasing power. No gains, no headway! Contrast that to a ten-year record on an equity mutual fund. There are many professionally managed equity mutual funds that would have provided you with a return in the order of 11% – 14% during the last ten years.

## Risk versus Reward Tradeoff

The chart below depicts a range of possible returns on different investments. In general terms, as you increase the degree of risk on the horizontal axis, so also do you increase the degree of reward on the vertical axis.

**Building An Investment Portfolio**

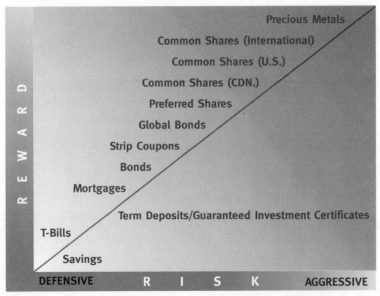

**Risk** is measured in terms of volatility —

how far an investment or class of invest-

ments swing up or down; an investor's focus

should be on the **whole** portfolio, not

the individual investment or asset class.

▶ **Asset allocation** rests on managing risk,

not picking winners. ▶ Regardless of how

much money you have, wisdom has to be

bought on the installment plan. ▶

Canada was built with sweat-equity and

**risk capital** (ownership), not

**savings accounts** and **term deposits**.

# thirteen

## Risk Versus Reward

**13**

**O**ne of the secrets of most successful investors is that they clearly understand their investment personality and their comfort zone with respect to risk.

**Investment Pyramid—Balancing Your Investment Strategy**

| Your Portfolio Objectives | Your Investment Personality | Degrees of Investment Risk/Reward |
|---|---|---|
| AGGRESSIVE GROWTH | RISK-TAKER | HIGH RISK/REWARD |
| MODERATE GROWTH AND INCOME | RISK-BLENDER | MODERATE RISK/REWARD |
| LOW GROWTH AND INCOME | RISK-MINIMIZER | LOW RISK/REWARD |
| RESERVES - INCOME INVESTMENTS | RISK-AVOIDER | VIRTUALLY NO RISK/REWARD |

As people build a portfolio, it helps to picture the investment structure in a pyramid and an inverse pyramid shape. The pyramid begins with a base of safe reserves and income investments. The central body of the pyramid contains growth and income investments for capital gains and dividends. The peak of the pyramid includes aggressive growth stocks, primarily to generate capital gains. Naturally, as people increase their degree of risk, they increase their potential reward proportionately. Lets take a closer look at the Investment Pyramid, which contains four levels of investment risk.

**Investment Pyramid**

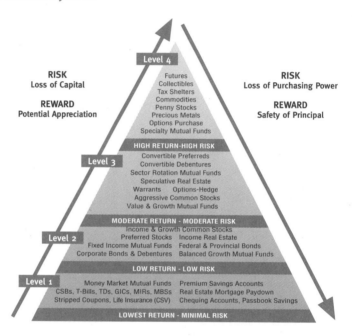

## Level 1: Risk-Avoider

The most conservative type of investors are risk-averse. Safety of capital is most important and risk of loss is to be minimized or avoided at all cost. In reality this person is not an investor at all; he or she is a saver. An investor is someone who looks forward to the future with faith; a saver is someone who looks backward into the past and is driven by fear.

A saver believes that a country's currency has real intrinsic value. Remember in Chapter 10 when we looked at Canadian stamp values and their loss of purchasing power. It is important to understand that saving has no economic benefit, only a psychological one. Historically, as a saver, the best one could hope for was a loss of purchasing power.

So how would you help a person who is a risk-avoider? You can't take them out of their comfort zone, therefore you can only exchange assets within their level of comfort. So for the risk-avoider, you would exchange assets from the right-hand side to the left-hand side at Level 1. For example Canadians hold tens of billions of dollars in chequing, passbook savings, and premium savings accounts, yielding zero to low single-digit returns in idle cash reserves. The key is to move this money into assets such as GICs and money market mutual funds that produce mid to higher single-digit returns.

## Level 2: Risk-Minimizer

This investor maintains a conservative stance towards investments but is comfortable with a small degree of risk. He or she understands that ownership investment principal will fluctuate, but over time can produce positive returns. Risk to the saver is the change in price or in the number of units he or she has. The risk minimizer equates risk with principal loss. The investor, however, understands that while principal loss might occur Canadian stamp values and their loss of purchasing power will happen for sure to the saver.

## Level 3: Risk-Blender

This investor embraces it all, through a blend of products, including a good selection of common shares or equity mutual funds invested to achieve growth. He or she understands that great companies share all of their profits with the owners.

When you lend your money to a bank or trust you are paid a return or rent for the use of that money. For example, a bank might pay you 2.5% for the loan of your money and then relend the funds to another person who's buying a car on time at 8.9% financing. The spread on this loan is the bank's profit. If you believe this is a good business for a bank to be in, then why lend your money to the bank via a savings account? Why not own shares of the bank itself?

## Level 4: Risk-Taker

Very few people will find themselves at this level; the risk is just too high. As many as 85% of risk-takers get their knuckles rapped and lose money more often than they win.

Typically, 5% to 10% of investors will find their personalities are at the bottom or the top of the pyramid; while 80% to 90% will be in the mid groupings — risk-minimizers or risk-blenders. Each successive level allows the investor more choices; for example a Level 3 risk-blender can participate in all of the assets in the pyramid at Levels 1, 2, and 3.

Employees should be shown impartial evidence based on historical data on how the risk/reward relationship relates to their tolerance for risk. For instance, the risk of having all of their investments in reserves and guaranteed investments, which, over the long term, would not produce the investment assets necessary to provide a desirable pension benefit at retirement, would probably be made from an uninformed decision. However, if an employee were to skew asset allocation decisions towards reserves and guaranteed products a few years prior to retirement, so as not to risk a downturn in the equity market close to the employee's retirement date, it might indicate that the employee is operating from an informed base.

## Types of Risk

Risk and chance are two critical concepts an investor must learn to separate. Risk can be measured, based on the statistics of past performance; chance can not. There is always some degree of risk in everything. Life is not without risk. Successful financial planning involves taking some measured degree of risk.

In general, as investors increase their degree of risk, so also do they increase their potential reward. There is no such thing as a riskless investment; just different types and degrees of risk. For example, fixed income investments are subject to purchasing power risk (inflation) as well as interest rate risk (the value of the investment diminishing as interest rates rise), which are often greater than the market risk involved in a good professionally managed equity fund.

Empirical research shows a 60% equity to

40% bond ratio will enhance overall

return without increasing portfolio risk.

You have to venture beyond the savings

Strategic asset allocation studies by

mentality if you want financial success.

several different research groups

Invest in free enterprise — there is risk,

have shown that asset allocation can

but there is **reward**. Inflation and taxes

account for as much as 90% of results:

trample profit. You can "go broke safely" on

interest income, or you can **outpace** infla-

tion by adding strategic amounts of risk to

the asset mix in your investment portfolio.

| | |
|---|---|
| ASSET ALLOCATION | 90% |
| SECURITY SELECTION | 7% |
| MARKETING TIMING | 2% |
| OTHER | 1% |

# fourteen

## Asset Allocation Strategies

**14**

**T**here are four things you can do with financial advice once you receive it:

- Buy assets
- Sell assets
- Change title to assets
- Nothing

Without a financial strategy, you cannot make effective savings, investment, or asset allocation decisions. So how would you allocate your assets to the following categories?

**Asset Allocation**

|  |  | Your Personal Allocation | Typical Canadian Pension Fund |
|---|---|---|---|
| **Reserves** | Cash & Equivalents | _____ | 5% |
| **Debt** | Bonds & Fixed Income | _____ | 40% |
| **Equity** | Stocks & Equity Mutual Funds | _____ | 55% |
|  |  | 100% | 100% |

Typical Canadian pension funds have historically allocated about 45% to reserves and bonds and 55% to equities. Other countries have taken an even more aggressive approach. This has proven to be a sound formula for institutional pension fund managers, so why not consider this ratio as a good starting point for your personal asset allocation. Let's take a look at what has worked historically and model the success that these managers have been achieving for decades, based on the following principles:

- Consider the whole portfolio performance rather than individual investments.
- No investment is inherently prudent or imprudent — in fact, certain non-traditional investment vehicles may actually be prudent.
- Assets should be diversified across all asset classes and risk-reducing strategies should be employed to offset the ravages of inflation.
- Global markets may be considered as a strategy to both enhance performance and reduce risk.
- Merely achieving the preservation of capital is not sufficient — preserving capital is not the same as maintaining purchasing power.

Whatever your personal asset allocation choices are, 90% of the performance you obtain will be based on how you distribute your money to the three basic categories of reserves, debt, and equities.

Asset allocation is more important than investment selection

90% ASSET ALLOCATION

7% SECURITY SELECTION

2% MARKET TIMING

1% OTHER

The vast majority of investors concentrate all of their efforts on security selection and market timing, which together account for less than 10% of the asset allocation solution.

## The Triangle of Investment Objectives

Every sound financial plan should include focused goals:

These goals group together in a Triangle of Investment Objectives. On the bottom is safety. Safety to most investors implies assurety of an income flow and instant liquidity. On the top is growth. There are two types of growth: defensive and aggressive. Picture yourself somewhere within the centre of this triangle.

Investors should try not to be in any one point of the triangle. Rather, they should picture themselves towards the centre of the triangle, participating with an asset allocation strategy that blends a mix of investments to meet liquidity, income, and growth objectives.

For example, if you are one who has only Canada Savings Bonds in your portfolio, your emphasis is safety. You must understand clearly that by cowering in the lower area of the triangle for safety, you forgo opportunities in the upper area for growth. Try to balance your strategies. Get out of the restrictive safety net and start to participate with some growth in the defensive, and perhaps the aggressive, sectors of the triangle as well as in the income and liquidity sectors. You will then have a mixture that gives balanced performance.

## Portfolio Construction

Just as an architect drafts construction plans for a house, an investor constructs an investment portfolio. The mission is to design a portfolio mix tailored to fit the individual comfort zone. The eventual success of a portfolio depends on the asset mix and its tax implications. The asset mix chosen evolves from the three major investment objectives of liquidity, income, and growth. The three major asset classes of reserves, debt, and equity serve the investor very well in meeting the investment objective. And each of these asset classes accommodate a particular investment suitable for the purpose of measuring risk/reward and return on investments. While there are a myriad of investments to choose from the three investments we will use are T-Bills, bonds, and stocks.

**Major Objective, Asset Class, and Investment Selection**

| Major Objective | Asset Class | Investment Selection |
| --- | --- | --- |
| Liquidity | Reserves | T-Bills |
| Income | Debt | Bonds |
| Growth | Equity | Stocks |

## A Portfolio Model for All Seasons

Investment returns have been expanding, especially during the last two decades. Rarely, if ever, have we witnessed greater extremes with inflation, deficits, interest rates, risk premiums, and investment returns than during this period. Therefore, if we were making projections for the next few decades, the anticipated long-term returns could be as follows:

| Compound Investment | Annual Return |
| --- | --- |
| T-Bills | 6% |
| Bonds | 8% |
| Stocks | 12% |
| Inflation | 5% |

Numerous studies have proven that the return one expects to obtain is not determined primarily by security selection; rather asset allocation will factor largely into the result. Conclusion: It's better to own the wrong investment in the right asset class than the right investment in the wrong asset class. With this picture in mind, let's glance at the accompanying table and look at four possible asset allocation solutions designed to match the investor profiles.

The weighted portfolio returns range from 7.1% for a risk-avoider to 10.9% for a risk-taker. Obviously, rewards are higher for the risk-taker. Only you can decide how much risk you want to take with your money. Once you decide on this, the rest is simple.

## Typical Portfolio Weightings

| Investor Type | Investment | % of Portfolio | X | Expected Return | = | Weighted Return |
|---|---|---|---|---|---|---|
| RISK-AVOIDER | T-Bills | 65% | | 6% | | 3.9% |
| (very conservative) | Bonds | 25% | | 8% | | 2.0% |
| | Stocks | 10% | | 12% | | 1.2% |
| | Total Weighted Return | | | | | 7.1% |
| Risk-Minimizer | T-Bills | 45% | | 6% | | 2.7% |
| (conservative) | Bonds | 30% | | 8% | | 2.4% |
| | Stocks | 25% | | 12% | | 3.0% |
| | Total Weighted Return | | | | | 8.1% |
| Risk-Blender | T-Bills | 15% | | 6% | | .9% |
| (less conservative | Bonds | 30% | | 8% | | 2.4% |
| growth oriented) | Stocks | 55% | | 12% | | 6.6% |
| | Total Weighted Return | | | | | 9.9% |
| Risk-Taker | T-Bills | 5% | | 6% | | .3% |
| (high risk growth | Bonds | 20% | | 8% | | 1.6% |
| speculator) | Stocks | 75% | | 12% | | 9.0% |
| | Total Weighted Return | | | | | 10.9% |

Retirees today, need at least 75% of pre-retirement earnings; retirees in 2010 will need 100% of prior earnings to maintain their lifestyles because of clawbacks, higher taxes, surtaxes, withholding taxes, and increasing medical user fees. These events necessitate a more aggressive growth approach to asset allocation whereby retirees allocate as much as 50% in equities to maintain the growth in their portfolios well into their 70s. For most retirees, this is the only solution. Failure to allocate a substantial portion to equities will cause retirees to run out of money before they run out of retirement.

Over a 35-year career an increase in the

annual rate of return of $1\%$ on your pension

fund will deliver a pension payout that's

**20**% greater at retirement. The corner-

stone to a good long-term financial plan

is diversification. The people on the

Forbes annual list of the top 400 wealthi-

est in the world all made their

money in one of two ways: ownership of

companies and ownership of real estate.

The key formula is to model their success!

# fifteen

## Investment Selection Strategies

**15**

**M**any employees make terrible investment choices and lean too heavily towards reserves and guaranteed income. By placing the majority of their assets in low-risk, low-return investments, they are ensuring that they won't have enough money at retirement. Our goal is to build the employee's investment skill level and confidence.

So what type of investments are needed to acquire the pension assets you'll need at retirement? Equities should account for as much as 55% or more of your portfolio, similar to what an institutional pension manager would allocate. Anything less than 55% in equities may force you to work a few extra years before retiring.

Many employees estimate their retirement needs, but forget that the value of their savings will depreciate over time if not invested for capital appreciation. They forget about inflation and, at the same time they are saving for retirement, they might also be paying off a mortgage, financing their children's college education, or helping an aging parent in an eldercare situation.

## Building Your Investment Portfolio

As you build a portfolio, you start out with interest-sensitive vehicles such as savings deposits, CSBs, and T-Bills. This is the base that provides a solid foundation. Then you might add a layer of preferred shares, which are essentially income vehicles; then a layer of dividend-paying common shares for growth and income. Finally, add shares for aggressive growth, plus a capstone of assorted other security types such as gold, warrants, or options, if they meet your tolerance for risk.

Build your structure over time depending on the risk/reward ratio you want to assume. Construct your portfolio to fit your comfort zone. As you increase your degree of risk, you may lose some of your capital, but your minor losses will be more than offset by your increased reward potential in all but the most severe cases.

There are two specific strategies to consider; one for fixed income and one for equities, both of which could add substantial performance to your pension and investment portfolios.

## Investment Strategy #1 — Fixed Income

On your fixed income investments such as GICs, stagger the maturities. Quite often the difference between one-year and five-year GIC rates vary between 1% and 2 1/2%. When people try to guess where rates are headed they inevitably guess wrong! We saw earlier that market timing only accounts for 2% of your long-term performance results. Therefore, it's best to allocate long-term GIC positions as in the following table. Initially, you take your lump-sum dollars allocated for GICs and divide the pool into five equal parts staggered from one to five years. As each term matures, you'll always renew to the longest term so that you constantly maintain equal percentages. Over the long term, this strategy will produce superior returns because you'll always be purchasing the five-year GICs that offer the highest rate no matter what direction the overall economy is headed.

**Typical Spread On GIC Rates**

| 1Yr. | 2Yr. | 3Yr. | 4Yr. | 5Yr. |
|------|------|------|------|------|
| 3.50 | 4.25 | 4.50 | 5.00 | 5.50 |

**$25,000 — GICs**

Long Term Asset Allocation

| Step 1: Buy | 1Yr. Term | $5000 |
|-------------|-----------|-------|
|             | 2Yr. Term | $5000 |
|             | 3Yr. Term | $5000 |
|             | 4Yr. Term | $5000 |
|             | 5Yr. Term | $5000 |

Step 2: **Roll over 20% of GICs Into New 5-Year Term Each Year**

## Investment Strategy #2 — Equities

So many investors have had a bad experience with one or two stocks that it has left them with a negative attitude about the whole concept of ownership. And yet one of the only ways you can increase your real wealth is to own equities. The best way to turn this negative experience around is to diversify your assets. Let's illustrate this by introducing you to two typical clients:

Client A — has a Risk-Avoider personality and is content to invest in cash reserves and fixed-income investments. Lets assume Client A invests $10,000 at 6% for 20 years. Net result $32,100.

Client B — has a Risk-Minimizer personality and decides to allocate $10,000 to equities. With the help of an advisor, Client B divides the $10,000 into five equal parts of $2,000. Twenty years later Client B decides to review the performance of the equities. One investment lost everything, including the original capital; another earned a very paltry 1% return; the other three produced returns of 8%, 10%, and 14% for 20 years. Net result $52,700.

## Safety By Diversification

Client A — Risk-Avoider (TDs, GICs, Savings Accounts)

| | |
|---|---|
| $10,000 @ 6% for 20 years | $ 32,100 |

Client B — Risk-Minimizer (Diversified Equity)

| | |
|---|---|
| $2,000 @ 0% for 20 years | $ 0 |
| $2,000 @ 1% for 20 years | $ 2,440 |
| $2,000 @ 8% for 20 years | $ 9,320 |
| $2,000 @ 10% for 20 years | $ 13,460 |
| $2,000 @ 14% for 20 years | $ 27,480 |
| | $ 52,700 |
| Insurance Premium = | $ 20,600 |

Even though Client B had two investments out of five that bombed, the other three carried the overall performance to a level that far surpassed Client A's total return.

## Insurance Premium

How much are you paying the Canadian Deposit Insurance Corporation (CDIC) in insurance premiums? Most Canadians hold substantial deposits at the banks, trusts, and brokerage companies. Do you know what the third letter in CDIC stands for? INSURANCE! Now we all know that to buy insurance we must pay a **PREMIUM**. Do you know what the premium is for the CDIC insurance that provides the safety of your investment in term deposits or guaranteed investment certificates? In this example, the premium is $20,600 which is the difference in the performance between the two portfolios.

In this example five individual stocks were purchased. In fact, for most investors, using a packaged money approach such as mutual funds is recommended. Had we used this type of allocation the net difference in the two portfolios might have been substantially greater. Let's take a look at Client B's portfolio using equity mutual funds. What return might he or she expect to get? While its possible to lose all of your money in a singular stock, it's almost impossible to lose all of your money in a diversified portfolio invested in many different companies in different industries.

Let's replace the two non-performing stocks with two good quality mutual funds. Substitute a 12% return for 20 years in place of the 0% and 1% returns. Now the premium increases to $56,760, which is the difference between Client A and Client B.

| Client A —Risk-Avoider (TDs, GICs, Savings Accounts) | |
|---|---|
| $10,000 @ 6% for 20 years | $ 32,100 |

| Client B —Risk-Minimizer (Mutual Funds) | |
|---|---|
| $2,000 @ 12% for 20 years | $ 19,300 |
| $2,000 @ 12% for 20 years | $ 19,300 |
| $2,000 @ 8%  for 20 years | $  9,320 |
| $2,000 @ 10% for 20 years | $ 13,460 |
| $2,000 @ 14% for 20 years | $ 27,480 |
| | $ 88,860 |
| Insurance Premium = | $ 56,760 |

What mindset does Client A have that directs all of the investments towards a very conservative fixed-income approach? Client A is driven by the guarantee provided by the CDIC and as a result has paid a substantial premium for that conservative approach.

Every time you purchase stocks or equity mutual funds you carry greater risks in your portfolio, but the rewards will far outweigh the risks over time if you constantly maintain a diversified approach to your investments. Typically, every time you invest in ten transactions by stock, industry, or country, you might expect this result: win 6, neutral 2, lose 2. The 60% in the win column will inevitably cover the other 40% and then some.

Birth of **mutual funds** in Canada — **1931**.

Net assets of mutual funds December 31,

"Just as there is no perfect person, painting,

**1982** — **$4** Billion. Net assets of mutual funds

or poem, so there is no perfect investment.

December 31, **1996** — **$212** Billion.

But the one that comes the closest for most

**One-third** of Canadians have no savings

people is the mutual fund."

or **investment program** for retirement.

— Money magazine

Some may not be able to **afford** to

FROM 1969 TO 1994 THE TEMPLETON GROWTH FUND PRODUCED:

retire. Money knows no boundaries. You

**17.5%** IF YOU BOUGHT AT THE HIGHEST POINT OF EACH CYCLE.

vote with your pocketbook. When you

**18.3%** IF YOU BOUGHT AT THE LOWEST POINT OF EACH CYCLE.

purchase a **foreign** mutual fund, you

The **0.8%** DIFFERENCE IN PERFORMANCE PROVES THE FOLLOWING:

are casting your vote for the company

**TIME** IS MORE IMPORTANT THAN TIMING

and the currency of **that country.**

THE **BEST TIME** TO INVEST IS WHEN YOU HAVE THE MONEY.

# sixteen

## Mutual Funds

**16**

**A** mutual fund is a pre-selected investment portfolio, chosen by a professional money manager(s), sponsored by an investment management company, and sold to the public as a single financial product in the form of units. A mutual fund allows you to join with other investors to secure advantages such as professional management and portfolio diversification that would not be generally available to you as an individual. Mutual funds are the answer for 90% of the investing population who lack the time and knowledge to make their own sound investment decisions in today's complex markets.

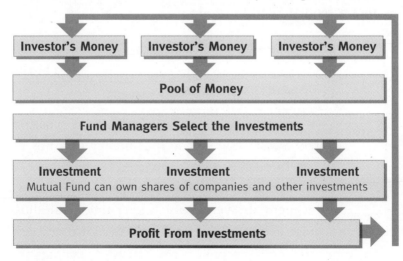

Investor's Money    Investor's Money    Investor's Money

Pool of Money

Fund Managers Select the Investments

Investment    Investment    Investment
Mutual Fund can own shares of companies and other investments

Profit From Investments

## Segregated Funds

Pension assets are a type of mutual fund, which are often referred to as pooled or segregated funds. Pension funds generally have much lower management and trustee fees and offer a much more conservative approach to investing than publicly traded mutual funds.

## Mutual Funds — The Major Benefits

There are many benefits to be derived from investing in mutual funds such as professional management, safety, liquidity, diversification, and the potential performance that a well-chosen fund can provide. Numerous other benefits of mutual fund investments include: convenience and simplicity, tax advantages, inflation hedge, lower costs, track records, reinvestment privileges, exchange privileges, elimination of timing decisions, systematic withdrawal plans, collateral, safekeeping, and ease of estate planning.

## Building a Mutual Fund Portfolio

There are well over 1200 Canadian mutual funds available to investors with many different objectives and a broad range of investments to choose from.

Each successive level on the matrix increases your risk/reward potential. You can invest your money in funds in a lump sum or through periodic payments on a monthly or quarterly basis. Regular periodic investing is one of the most effective investment strategies, which over time, will allow you to acquire more units when prices are down and fewer units

## Building a Mutual Fund Portfolio

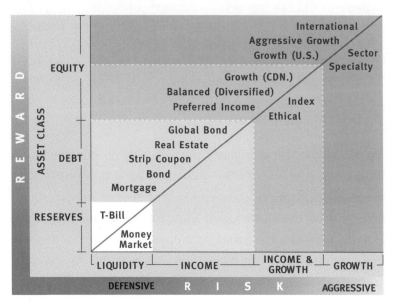

when prices are high. This strategy is called dollar cost averaging. Let's take a look at how it works:

### Dollar Cost Averaging

|         | Investment | Price Per Unit | Units Bought |
|---------|-----------|----------------|--------------|
| Month 1 | $100.00   | $10.00         | 10.000       |
| Month 2 | 100.00    | 6.00           | 16.666       |
| Month 3 | 100.00    | 9.00           | 11.111       |

In Month 1, a regular periodic investment of $100 at a current unit price of $10 will enable the investor to buy 10 units. In Month 2, the market price has declined by 40% from $10 to $6 per unit; therefore, the periodic investment of $100 will buy 16.666 units. Just like any other sale, you get more units (value) when the price is lower. In Month 3, the market price has recovered to $9 per unit. That month the periodic investment of $100 will buy 11.111 units. The 3 month summary is as follows:

| | | |
|---|---|---|
| Total cost | | $ 300.00 |
| Units purchased | | 37.777 |
| Current price | | $ 9.00 |
| Current value of investment | | $ 340.00 |
| Capital gain (loss) | 13.3% | $ 40.00 |
| Increase (decrease) in unit value | (10.0%) | $ 1.00 |

## Mutual Funds Offer Diversification

No individual, no company, no industry, no country, is an island. We live in a global universe that is becoming more impatient, with fierce competition and fleeting opportunities. Each passing day, individuals must become more lean, agile, and quick to seize the investment opportunities that will come their way. Investors can select their own portfolio investments or they may choose mutual funds to provide a measure of safety by dividing investment dollars into a wide cross-section of securities. This would be impossible to do on your own without the benefit of having millions of dollars to invest. With mutual funds, instead of putting all of their eggs in a few baskets, investors are able to enjoy the benefits of many baskets. Depending on their size, mutual funds generally hold anywhere from 30 to 300 different securities in many industries.

There are four major categories of diversification:

1 **By type of fund assets**
2 **By investment selection**
3 **By countries and currencies**
4 **By managerial styles**

## Management Styles

Professional money managers have different managerial styles. The three basic styles are: value, growth, and market timers. It is important to understand how different managers approach investments and how different funds, even if managed by the same company, can provide different results. At any point in time, one managerial style will outperform another, but over the long-term, every style has its merits. Often a blended portfolio of several funds encompassing different managerial styles will produce the best results.

## How to Select a Professionally Managed Fund Manager

There are several things an investor should consider when selecting a money manager.

■ The investor generally chooses a management company based on past performance and proven management track record.

■ Most management companies have a family of funds from which to choose.

■ The investor selects a fund that fits his or her needs and objectives in concert with the individual's level of risk tolerance.

■ Each professionally managed mutual fund has a money manager(s) who is responsible for the day-to-day operation and overall performance of the fund.

It is important to know that a typical money manager is:

■ compensated on performance

■ paid a salary and usually a performance bonus

■ not commission driven

■ results oriented, since his or her job is on the line and investment decisions are reviewed usually on a monthly or quarterly basis

■ a full-time professional involved with investment selection

The daily issue of *The Globe and Mail,* Report on Business section contains more information than the average person would acquire in a lifetime just four centuries ago. Today we have a new kind of employee emerging who is better educated than in the past, more conscious of the need to be financially responsible at an earlier age, and inundated with more financial information, options, and decisions than at any other time. The merits of load versus no-load mutual funds should be looked at as the concept of advice or no advice. Which would you prefer?

"With the invention of the computer, our information supply is doubling every 5 years. Microchips are doubling in performance power every 18 months."

– Strategic Coach

# seventeen

## Choosing A Financial Planner

**17**

**I**nvestment knowledge and skills can become outdated very quickly. Computerized trading programs and a myriad of other sophisticated institutional tools and knowledge-based information systems all but eliminate any chance of a level playing field for the novice retail investor. A dedicated lifelong investment-learning program would offer the only chance for survival in the institutionalized investment markets today.

Most investors entrust their investments to a professional stockbroker, mutual fund specialist, investment advisor, or financial planner; someone who is dedicated to the preservation and growth of their capital. For some people, however, this is not the answer.

Do you have what it takes to make buy and sell decisions at the appropriate time, or would a professional money manager be the solution for you?

To assist you with this decision, rank yourself on the Four Major Ingredients for Self-Management. Upon completion, you should have a pretty good idea of whether you should engage the services of a planner or go it alone.

## Four Major Ingredients for Self-Management

| | Professional Management | | | Self Management | | |
|---|---|---|---|---|---|---|
| Time | 0 | 1 | 2 | 3 | 4 | 5 |
| Knowledge | 0 | 1 | 2 | 3 | 4 | 5 |
| Temperament | 0 | 1 | 2 | 3 | 4 | 5 |
| Money | 0 | 1 | 2 | 3 | 4 | 5 |

**Time** — Do you have three, four, or five hours to spend every day after your busy workday to read and research information and data? Or would you rather spend your time pursuing leisure interests, sports, recreation, or perhaps some quality time with family or friends. If you do have a lot of time to study and analyze the markets, score yourself higher; if you don't have the time or choose not to spend it pursuing financial and investment planning score yourself lower.

**Knowledge** — Do you have adequate training and knowledge about the stock market and other investment issues? Rank yourself accordingly.

**Temperament** — Every single investment decision is made in a gray area — it's never black or white. Whether you are buying or selling, at a gut level you'll find yourself asking, "Is this the right decision?" It's never easy. If it was easy we would all be doing it. Where do you think you rank on temperament?

**Money** — Do you have substantial dollars to work with to provide ample diversification? Individual stock investments should normally be made in $5,000 increments to minimize the effect of brokerage commissions. Often full service brokerages charge minimum commissions of $75 to $85 per transaction. If you were investing $100 per month on a pre-authorized chequing plan, you would need a form of investing whereby all or most of the $100 was invested. Where would you rank yourself based on your total money available for investment?

## Scoring Results

**17-20 points**

You've got what it takes to manage your financial plan. You know how to set goals and implement investment strategies to fulfill your needs and objectives.

**12-16 points**

You are well on your way. You know what your goals are, but you are not sure about implementing them on your own. You require the services of an investment advisor or a financial planner who understands your needs and objectives. Your investment strategies may take a self-managed approach with professional guidance from your investment advisor, or it may include professionally managed mutual funds.

**0-11 points**

You, along with 90% of investors, should consider professional money management. You need help in establishing your goals, and you require the assistance of an investment advisor, a financial planner, or other professional counsellor to implement your plan for you. A combination of adequate reserves to match your selection of professionally managed mutual funds will allow you to accomplish your investment objectives, and provide you with financial independence in the future.

## Who Are Professional Financial Planners?

Historically, there have been four pillars of finance in Canada — banks, trust companies, insurance companies, and investment dealers. As people like you continue to forge your own financial future, the old pillars must have increased flexibility to meet the demand. As a result, these institutions have begun vying for each other's business. Banks want to get into the investment business. Trust companies want to perform more banking services. Investment dealers want to get in the insurance business, and on it goes. Out of these various disciplines, the professional financial planner has emerged.

A financial planner may be a stockbroker, accountant, lawyer, insurance agent, or pension/benefit consultant. Most genuine financial planners were once associated with one of the above professions. In their role as financial planners, each tends to lean on the discipline from which they evolved. The financial planner is a generalist with broad financial training and experience in areas such as saving and investment strategies, income tax planning, accounting, of wills and estates, and insurance and disability security as well as the awareness of shifting tides in our economy, finance, and politics.

## How to Select Your Investment Advisor

How do you choose the right advisor to help you accomplish your investment goals? Remember, next to your number one asset — your physical health, you are dealing with a very important asset — your financial health, and you cannot afford to make a major mistake.

If you decide to hire a professional planner, develop a relationship with one principal advisor, someone you can trust. Most investors would rather conduct their investing and financial planning with one person than with several. Deal with someone who understands your personal needs, who is not product-oriented, who is not commission-oriented, and who will provide service and follow-through.

## Guidelines for Selecting a Financial Planner

Whoever your principal advisor may be, the key is to find a planner who possesses the traits and characteristics mentioned on the next page and who makes you feel comfortable. The following is representative of the want list of our participants and has been compiled from our seminars and workshops.

## Financial Planner Characteristics

| | |
|---|---|
| Honest | Good listener |
| Sincere | Sensitive |
| Trustworthy | Speaks in lay terms |
| Explains my options clearly | Friendly |
| Good rapport | Age compatibility |
| Firm but not aggressive | Experienced |
| Versatile | Proven track record |
| Accessible | Past performance |
| Returns calls promptly | Outstanding client references |
| Referrals | Affordable |
| Good personal background | Independent |
| Empathy for my goals | Unbiased |
| Good advice | Similar client profiles to mine |
| Full disclosure | Respected by peers |
| Confidentiality | Support staff |
| Chemistry | Specialist network |
| Approachable | Resources |
| Knowledgeable | Frequent review of financial plan |
| Personality compatible with mine | Supply regular newsletters |
| Service and results oriented | Constant upgrade of skills |
| Keeps me informed | Does he or she represent one |
| Global investor | family of funds or many? |
| Formal education | What's in it for me? |
| How much can he or she save me? | How compensated? |
| Bonded business & financial | Is the initial meeting free? |
| credentials such as: B. Comm., | What has he or she done |
| F.C.S.I., C.F.P., R.F.P., C.L.U. | for me lately? |

If you were to summarize this list and you only had one thing to go on, which would you choose? Probably a reference or referral would be the number one choice. Someone you know well and respect, refers you to someone they have had a good relationship with would be a great place to start. The only provision would be that the relationship had matured over several years — long enough to have experienced a complete market cycle of ups and downs. That way you're not being referred to someone who thinks the world of their planner, based on a short-term relationship in a hot market when, in fact, virtually every planner looks like a hero. Only a relationship that can withstand the inevitable bear market corrections measured over a complete cycle should be looked at seriously.

## In the Office With Your Financial Planner

The initial meeting with your planner involves a data gathering and needs analysis session to assess your relationship. Before a planner can coach you he or she must know as much about you as you are willing to divulge.

Your planner must be a good listener and will instinctively know what questions to ask you in order to solicit as much information as possible on the following subjects:

| | |
|---|---|
| Your Current Age/Stage in Life | Power of Attorney |
| Dependents | Tax Bracket |
| Relationship Stability | Net Worth |
| Career Security | Equity Exposure |
| Current Income | Debt Structure |
| Prospects for Higher Income | Economic Environment |
| Retirement Funding | Education Funding |
| Will and Estate | Tolerance for Risk |

## Working With Your Financial Planner

Most people think that creating a financial plan is complex. It isn't. From the checklist above only three items of information are necessary:

1 **What you own and what you owe**

2 **What you earn and what you spend**

3 **What standard of living you hope to have when you retire**

The financial planner first determines all of the above and then calculates what you must save and what your investments should earn over the next year to be on track. He or she than advises you on specific investments and savings plans that match your comfort zone with respect to risk. It's that simple!

Achieving financial success doesn't end with paying your money to a personal financial planner and foregoing any further responsibility. Once you have established a financial plan, you must be committed to it. The following checklist can help you keep on track.

1. **Stay committed to your plan.**
2. **Communicate fully with your advisor.**
3. **Be honest with your advisor.**
4. **At the data-gathering stage, provide all the information you can, not bits and pieces, otherwise you may have to redo the plan.**
5. **Don't be afraid to ask questions if you don't understand.**

## Fees and Commissions

Basically, there are three ways to work in the financial planning industry. Some financial planners are "fee only," some "commission only," and some "fee plus commission." In the brokerage business, there are some products that have commission and some that don't. In the insurance industry, there are higher commissions on some types of products than others. But in almost every scenario there is a commission or a fee to contend with. Many times the fee or commission is hidden; that is, it is built into the offering price on the product.

Many financial planners may introduce products by giving you a financial plan, which has no cost if you buy their products. But it does have a cost whereby they charge you a fee if you do not purchase their product. Similarly, with accountants and lawyers, the meter is running, generally speaking, from the moment you sit down to do business. In other words, if you spend an hour of their time, the meter is running and you are paying an hourly fee for that time.

In general, today, most people want the maximum amount of service for the least cost. Try to be reasonable in terms of your expectations. And always remember you have to invest a dollar to make a dollar.

The outlook for retirement in Canada today is

cloudy . Millions of Canadians will enter

retirement, **financially** and **psychologi-**

**cally** unprepared . Government may not be

able to ensure the financial needs of retirees

because there will be many more people

drawing on government support at a time

when the workforce that contributes the bulk

of tax revenue is shrinking . Ironically, those

employees who are in the best position to

retire have the least desire to do so; they

are driven and enjoy the race too **much.**

# eighteen

## Where Do You Go From Here?

**Y**our personal success depends on planning to attain financial dignity in your retirement. We define dignity as doing what you want, when you want, where you want, and with whom you want. To do that, you must specify your needs, estimate your income requirements, analyse your resources, select your investments, and do an annual financial check-up to make sure your retirement plans stay on course.

You must determine your personal goals, including anticipating the psychological roadblocks to happiness such as boredom and loss of self-esteem. Identifying satisfying leisure activities will enable you to combat these threats. Paying attention to your relationships with significant others can help you to retain emotional health, just as an exercise and nutritional program will keep you physically fit. The keys to success are avoiding procrastination and maintaining a winning attitude.

By now you realize it is not important what your net worth is today whatever your age. Cash flow is the lifeblood of the individual and putting aside a percentage right off the top by **"paying yourself first"** is the key to your future financial success. You know without a doubt that if you put money aside it is going to make money and the money that the money makes is going to make you some more money. That's the formula — a regulated employer's pension plan, a disciplined approach to RRSP investments, or both, with a commitment to **"pay yourself first"** every week for the rest of your life.

## Winning Mental Attitude

Let's review some of the major issues we've discussed:

- A winning mental attitude will enable you to retire with financial dignity.
- Wealth is created by utilizing time and money and by the magic of compounding.
- Time is your greatest ally; your very best friend.
- Think in blocks of time: ten, fifteen, twenty, thirty years into the future.
- An investment plan does not stop at age 65.
- Calculate the measurement of risk versus reward.
- Find investments that fit your risk tolerance.
- Excellent returns are attainable without having to take substantial risk.
- Life goes on and it is to be lived to the fullest into your retirement years.
- Happiness is arriving; the joy is in the journey.

## Taking Action — It's Your Move!

Here are some action steps you might consider taking:

- Attend "free" seminars.
- Take courses in "how to invest" (community college or by correspondence).
- Subscribe to specialty financial newsletters.

- Join an investment club.
- Read the financial section of your daily newspaper.
- Track the performance of a few selected mutual funds.
- Read financial planning books such as "Financial Pursuit".
- Ask friends and colleagues who they invest with.
- Establish a relationship with a financial planner.
- Collect personal and family data and have a financial plan drawn up.

Remember, there are three kinds of people in life:

# Those who make things happen.

# Those who watch things happen.

# Those who say "what happened"?

Above all, remember, **you can choose** your financial and lifestyle outcomes.

# FKI

## Specialists in Financial and Pre-retirement Education

### SEMINARS ♦ WORKSHOPS ♦ TRAINING

*Distributors of the Andex Chart for Canadian Investors*

## TOPICS

Financial Planning
Setting Goals
Designing Action Plans
Developing a Positive Attitude
Handling Procrastination
Power of Compounding
Paying Yourself First
Cash Management
Designing Statements
Tax Planning
Asset Allocation Strategies
Mutual Funds
Selecting a Financial Planner
Employer Pension Plans

Social Security Plans
RRSPs
Annuities, RRIFs, and LIFs
Will and Estate Planning
Housing and Real Estate
Maximizing Use of Leisure Time
Second Careers
Volunteerism
Travel
Wellness Issues
Relationships
Creating a Vital Retirement Lifestyle
Retiring With Financial Dignity

# Financial Knowledge Inc.

## Education Programs

**Financial Knowledge Inc's.** education programs address the needs of employees to learn:

• financial self-management skills & techniques

• career transition and lifestyle planning

• lifetime investment strategies

• pre-retirement planning.

Program formats are workshop, seminar, self-study, and train-the-trainer. Instruction and materials focus on financial self-management and making lifestyle changes for a rewarding and secure future. Our workshops use active participation by employees and spouses in developing personal goals for investing, retirement, and lifestyle planning.

## Customization— Made to Measure

At **Financial Knowledge Inc. (FKI)** we can tailor a program to suit your needs. We offer several standard programs however, upon request we can design to your goals. And our trainers have the maturity and financial industry experience you would expect, to deliver this sensitive subject matter to your employees.

You may already be offering financial, lifestyle, and/or pre-retirement planning programs to your employees and you may want to take a serious look at revamping an old program or you might be looking for an new pre-retirement program to enhance your benefits program. Whatever your need, we would be happy to provide a solution to fit your corporate culture. Perhaps it's time to take a new look at retirement...your employees' future well-being may depend on it.

**FKI**

# Financial Knowledge Inc.

## CORPORATE SEMINAR & WORKSHOP OUTLINES

Our goals are to educate participants in the lifetime skills of financial self-management; to motivate the individual to take action to secure a rewarding future; and to provide the tools and strategies needed to achieve financial independence and a fulfilling retirement.

**4-Hour Pension Transition Seminar** to enhance employee awareness and understanding of pension options; to focus on the employees responsibility of choosing the appropriate asset classes to fit their needs:

- risk tolerance profiles
- asset allocation strategies
- inflation (purchasing power)
- investment selection.

**1-Day Financial Planning Workshop** to address the following type of needs:

- financial self-management skills and techniques
- investment and asset allocation strategies
- pre-retirement preparation and planning
- creating a happy, healthy, lifestyle.

**2-Day Financial & Lifestyle Planning Workshop** in addition to the topics covered in the 1-Day Financial Planning Workshop covers many other topics such as:

- lifestyle and wellness issues
- human support systems
- attitudes towards retirement
- personal fulfillment
- utilization of time
- six powers of success.

**2-Day Downsizing and Early Leave Workshop** covers all of the topics in the 2-Day Financial and Lifestyle Planning Workshops as well as:

- career transition, challenges, and opportunities
- surviving severance and measuring options
- cash management strategies (short term versus long term)
- income tax strategies.

## Downsizing & Early Retirement Workshops

Our workshops provide an integral part of staff reduction and early retirement programs for *departing employees and the survivors!* We address the issues of wellness and lifestyle changes in all retirement planning programs.

**Career Transition** programs focus on wealth management and the *personal opportunities presented by change.*

**Surviving Severance** programs are excellent for *addressing cash management issues, assessing severance options, and applying income tax strategies.*

## Financial Self-Management & Pension Transition Workshops

We facilitate ongoing employee education programs. For example, sponsors of "money purchase" pension plans and employee directed savings and capital accumulation plans use our **Financial Pursuit** training to teach employees *asset allocation strategies/investing skills* for plan investments and personal wealth.

## Unbiased Advice — Fee Based

Our programs provide *unbiased generic education,* with no product affiliation (investment, insurance, or retirement services). Financial education is provided by trained and experienced professionals in our workshops with optional individual counselling available. We are compensated on a *fee for service basis.*

Presentations are sponsored by employers for groups of employees, by professional advisors for their clients, and by professional associations for their members.

# Financial Knowledge Inc.

## PUBLIC SEMINAR OUTLINE

Graydon Watters and Vorg Incorporated are pleased to announce the availability of the *Financial Survival for the 21st Century Seminar* based on the best-selling book by the same title. The seminar always provides a current viewpoint on the markets and where to invest your money now and stresses the following major topics:

### 3 Major Paradigm Shifts

- A New Paradigm for Retirement is Required
- FKI's Projections — Next 20 Years
- The Retirement Gap

### 6 Powers of Success

- Physical Health, Personal Control, Personal Skills, Personal Fulfillment, Precious Relationships, Pursuit of Financial Freedom
- Retirement 20st Century — Balanced Lifestyle 21st Century
- The Road to Retirement

### 6 Major Resources at Retirement

- Canada's Debt — NIMBY
- OAS/CPP Privileged or Entitled
- Political Games — High Human Cost

### Only 2 Ways to Increase Your Real Wealth

- Rehearse Your Life Plan
- Your Financial Planning Factory
- Time (86,400 seconds)
- Investment Personality Pyramid

### 4 Major Reasons Financial Plans Fail

- Procrastination
- Laws of Attitude
- Train of Life

### 4 Phases of Every Cycle

- Interest Rates — Stock Prices
- Investment Risks Can Effect Your Cruise
- Investment Cycle
- Ibbotson & Associates — After Taxes and Inflation
- The Stock Market Has Been Going Up All of Your Life
- Where is The Market Now?
- World Investment Opportunities

### Only 1 Asset Allocation Solution Matters

- Your Asset Allocation Solution

### Only 2 Ways to Manage Money

- Mutual Funds (Professional Versus Self-Management)
- Financial Advisors Add Value
- Relationships Don't Rust

---

*For more information on our corporate and public seminars and workshops please contact:*

*Jack Wright or Andy Billesdon*
**FINANCIAL KNOWLEDGE INC.**
279 Yorkland Blvd., North York, Ontario, M2J 1S7
Tel: (416) 499-5466  Fax: (416) 499-7748

# FINANCIAL SURVIVAL

for the

## 21st Century

*Perhaps the greatest gift that you could give to someone else is their own personal copy of* **Financial Survival for the 21st Century**. *The book makes a great gift for those significant others in your life: son, daughter, niece, nephew, friend, or business associate.* **Financial Survival for the 21st Century** *is the perfect resource for all Canadians from the time they begin their working careers until they retire.*

# Financial Product Order Form

| Quantity | Item Description | Regular Price | Net Price |
|----------|------------------|---------------|-----------|
| _____ | Financial Pursuit *(book)* | $   29.95 | $ _____ |
| _____ | Lifestyle Pursuit *(course)* | 245.00 | _____ |
| _____ | RRSP Calculator *(slide ruler)* | 4.00 | _____ |
| _____ | Andex Handout Chart *(16.5" x 11")* | 15.00 | _____ |
| _____ | Invest In Yourself *(audio cassettes **)* | 49.95 | _____ |
| _____ | Six Powers of Success *(Ruler**)* | 4.00 | _____ |
| _____ | Financial Survival for the 21st Century | 12.95 | _____ |
| _____ | *SPECIAL* COMPLETE PACKAGE *(one of each of the above)* | **299.00** | _____ |
| | **SUB TOTAL** | | $ _____ |
| | *SHIPPING & HANDLING* | | 7.00 |
| | *GST @ 7%* | | _____ |
| | *\*\*PST @ 8% (on audio cassettes and Six Powers of Success Ruler for Ontario Residents Only)* | | _____ |
| | **TOTAL** | | $ _____ |

*Please ship to*

Company Name: _____

Attention: _____

Address: _____

City: _____ Province: _____ Postal Code: _____

Telephone: (      ) _____ Fax: (      ) _____

*Method of Payment*

I have enclosed a cheque for $_____
made payable to Financial Knowledge Inc.

**OR**

Please debit my **VISA** or **MASTERCARD** in the amount $_____

Credit Card #:_____ Expiry Date:_____

Name of Cardholder: _____

Signature of Cardholder: _____

*WE OFFER DISCOUNTS FOR ORDERS OF 10 OR MORE ON OUR PRODUCTS. PLEASE WRITE, CALL, OR FAX FKI FOR DETAILS.*

## FINANCIAL KNOWLEDGE INC.

279 Yorkland Blvd., North York, Ontario, M2J 1S7    Tel: (416) 499-5466    Fax: (416) 499-7748

# Notes

........................................................................
........................................................................
........................................................................
........................................................................
........................................................................
........................................................................
........................................................................
........................................................................
........................................................................
........................................................................
........................................................................
........................................................................
........................................................................
........................................................................
........................................................................
........................................................................
........................................................................
........................................................................
........................................................................